Wing Chun Unchained

Unlocking Wing Chun's Potential

Tony Massengill

EFFICIENT WARRIOR
PUBLICATIONS

This book is dedicated to the memory of the greatest Wing Chun / Ving Tsun man I have ever met, Grandmaster Ip Ching
7/7/36 - 1/25/20

Acknowledgments

This is a book that has been several years in the making. Between my procrastination, coordination issues for photo shoots, and Covid ..... there have been many delays, but it is finally done!

Anytime a project like this is undertaken, there are many people to thank. So I would like to make the following attempt to thank those who have directly impacted this project or have indirectly impacted this project by way of their impact on my life both in and out of the martial arts. First of all I would like to thank God, and my Lord, Jesus Christ, who have saved me from what I deserve (Hell) and by grace have given me all of the blessings I have experienced in this life, and look forward to in the next!

I would like to thank my beautiful Wife, Yongnan for her love, understanding and support in my pursuit and training in the Science of Self-Protection.

I need to thank my teachers in the Ip Man lineage, Masters Edmund Fong and Samuel Kwok, who passed to me this great Wing Chun heritage.

I would like to say thank you to my Sigungs (Kung Fu Grandfathers) Grandmasters Ip Chun and Ip Ching (Sons of Grandmaster Ip Man), for their generous instruction in their father's Kung Fu method. Sadly, Ip Ching passed away before I could get this book anywhere near completion.

In the fifty plus years I have been involved in training in the Martial Arts there have been many people who have shared their knowledge with me, My first Wing Chun teacher, 1979 – 1984, Sifu Shiu Hung (Duncan) Leung, Ron Heimberger, Edmund Fong, Chu Sheung Tien, Siu Yuk Men, my classmate and choreographer of the first Ip Man movie, Leo Au Yeung, Wong Shung Leung Wing Chun instructor, David Peterson, among many others, thank you! I owe a special thank you to a man who has been my mentor, friend, counselor, and big brother, Glen Moore. Many people have taught me martial arts over the years, but it was Glen who taught me what it means to be a Warrior!

I would like to also say a special thank you to some of my students who have helped in many ways. So to Lafayette Harris, Jeff Benton, Jason Korol, Larry Harvey, Andrew Tate, Thomas Duncan and Antonio Parker.....Thank You! I am truly blessed by GOD to have all of these great people in my life!

Finally I wish to thank my pastor, Jeff Ferguson of Calvary Reformed Presbyterian Church, in Hampton Virginia, for his teaching and leadership.

And to my father in the Reformed Faith, R.C. Sproul ...... R.I.P.

Tony Massengill – 12/14/21

Foreword

by David Peterson

It is both an honour and a privilege to be asked to write a brief foreword to the volume that you now hold in your hands, written by my friend and fellow *Wing Chun* brother, *Sifu* Tony Massengill. As a teacher of *Wing Chun*, and as an author on the topic myself, I appreciate the amount of time and effort that goes into the writing of such a volume, not to mention the passion that I know *Sifu* Tony has put into not only the writing of this tome, but into a career in both law enforcement and the martial arts that spans a great many years.

We knew of each other for quite a long time, having interacted on the Internet and thru email on several occasions over the years, but only had the opportunity to meet face-to-face as recently as March in 2014 when, on the invitation of both *Sifu* Tony and *Sifu* Jason Korol, I was invited to conduct a seminar/workshop weekend on the *Wong Shun Leung Ving Tsun Kuen Hok* method at the 'Greenville Academy of Martial Arts' in South Carolina. Long story short, we all got along like the proverbial house on fire, enjoying a fantastic few days of talking, training, sharing and having fun!

Whilst we are not from the same *Wing Chun* lineage, we share the same passion for preserving and passing on this great legacy that we love, so while our interpretations of the system may not be exactly in synch, our shared desire to bring awareness to the brilliance that is *Wing Chun Gung-fu* is totally on par. During that brief visit in 2014, I found *Sifu* Tony to be a man totally open to new ideas and new methods, a man with a huge desire to seek out the very best ideas and methods to share with his students, and not some stuck-in-the-mud traditionalist who is trapped in a time warp.

I also found in *Sifu* Tony, a man who has a great deal of respect for the past, and for the great teachers of the past, and not just his own teachers! He has continued to demonstrate this respect with his constant references to my own teacher, the late *Sifu* Wong Shun Leung, and by extension to myself, by recommending his students acquaint themselves with my work on my late teachers methods. I cannot thank him enough for supporting my work in that way. Within this very volume the reader will see evidence of that openness to look outside of his own lineage, rather than take a more blinkered approach.

Within the pages of this book, he will challenge you to open your minds to the potential of *Wing Chun*, and to not be afraid to develop your skills such that you can make your *Wing Chun* a better fit for today's situations, rather than blindly clinging to old approaches to training and applications that do not equip us for the needs of the 21st century. The world has changed over the 300 or so years that *Wing Chun* has been around, and as practitioners of this system, we need to address those changes and free ourselves of outdated practices and ideas that prevent us from reaching our full potential.

Wing Chun Unchained is a book that every practitioner of the system should own and read, a book that will help to free you from the restraints that may have unconsciously prevented you from fully appreciating what *Wing Chun* can do, ...and what you can do with *Wing Chun*! As my late teacher was so fond of telling us, "You have to make *Wing Chun* your slave, and not let it become your master", to step outside the box and approach your training so as to maximise not only your own full potential, but to realise the full potential of *Wing Chun* as well. Read and re-read this book often – you won't regret it. Congratulations to *Sifu*

Foreword

Tony Massengill on a fine piece of writing which will help many people to make their *Wing Chun* truly *Unchained!*

David Peterson,
    Malaysia, 2020.

Introduction

There are times I really worry about how people will take my ideas.... and then there are times when I really don't care!. Actually the latter is how I am most of the time. I am a little controversial in my approach to Wing Chun, and I have a tendency to speak my mind a little too directly for some peoples taste. There are times I kick over some people's sacred cows, and times when I stomp on them after kicking them over. It's not my intention to be disrespectful or purposely controversial; I'm just not much of a politician!

As I write this, I recently celebrated my sixtieth birthday and have been a martial artist for over fifty-four of those years. I have trained and earned instructor certification or Black Belt rank in Tae Kwon Do, Kenpo, Kajukenbo, Stick & Knife Combatives, Chin-Na (Chinese Grappling) and Wing Chun. I have fought in non-contact as well as full-contact fights. I have cross trained with Western Boxers and grapplers.

My career in public safety had me working as a police officer, firefighter and emergency medic, from which I retired with 27 years of service from the city of Newport sides handed to them in these fights, well, ... in police work, they call that a clue! It's not that Wing Chun does not have the tools to be an extremely effective fighting system in the modern world, it's just that the method of applying those tools needs to be drug out of the 1950's!

With "Wing Chun Unchained" we hook a winch to Traditional Wing Chun and drag it out of the dark ages, into the light of modern application! I challenge everyone reading this book to ponder the points made here, consider the bondage we have experienced, both to the traditions of the system, and the bondage in which we have held the system to our own limiting ideas and preconceptions as to what we believe Wing Chun to be.

In closing, I want to say thank you for your consideration of what is written here. I feel strongly that we owe it to the masters of the past who fought to bring this great system to us, to make sure the system is not left weaker after it has passed through our hands to the next generation.

Tony Massengill 12/14/21

A quick Note from the Author

The reader may find some inconsistencies in the spelling of some of the Chinese terms in this book. I have found that in my personal notes I sometimes spell different terms in differing ways. The Chinese word for hand is Sao, which I, and others, sometimes spell Sau. It is like the name of the system, Wing Chun is sometimes spelled Ving Tsun. At issue is the spelling of terms in the way they sound to the English speaker.

After reading this book, you will see that I have a hard enough time with the English language, so please don't fault me for my Chinese!

And speaking of my English...... Should the reader find themselves drawn beyond their ability to control, to make corrections to my gammer, punctuation and other mistakes I make in my writing, please make those corrections, In red ink, in your personal copy of this book or if you have the Kindle edition, go ahead and purchase a paperback and make those corrections, and mail it to:

Tony Massengill
P.O. Box 44612

Hampton, Virginia 23666

That way, I get the corrections you have made, and if after mailing your copy to me, you remember that aside from my writing errors, there was some pretty solid information in this book you would like to keep as a reference source, you can log onto Amazon and order another copy!

I like the sound of that!!

Thanks

Tony Massengill

Chapter 1

Where are you Headed

Have you ever started out on a trip to a destination, but didn't know how to get there? Imagine if you will, that my wife decides that we are going to take a trip to SeaWorld in Orlando, Florida. We pack up the bags with everything we think we will need for the trip. Secure the house, hop in the car and head from Hampton, Virginia to sunny Florida!

After we have been on the road for about three hours my wife asks me if we will be passing anywhere near Atlanta on the trip, to which I reply "I have no idea". To which she says "What"? And I repeat "I have no idea". At which time, she looks at me with those gorgeous brown eyes and says "How in the wide blue hell could you have no idea"? I reply "I didn't look at a map, I just hopped in the car and pointed the front bumper in the direction of Florida and stepped on the gas pedal"

She gives me that loving " Your hair didn't fall out, it fell in and clogged your brain" look that I see way too often and asks me " if you didn't look at a map before we left, and we don't have a GPS, how are you going to know which exits to

1

take and what route to follow"? To which I respond "I don't, I figure we will know when we have arrived when we see the big SeaWorld sign".

I know ..... stupid story, I mean really, who would take a trip, with no idea of how to get to the destination? Well, when you think about it, that is exactly how most journeys in the martial arts occur! In many cases it's even worse, many people not only have no idea how to get to their destination, they wander aimlessly, not even knowing what the destination is!

In that great American classic "Alice in Wonderland" Alice comes to a fork in the road, and doesn't know which direction to proceed. She sees the Cheshire Cat on a limb in a near-by tree and the following conversation begins:

"Alice: Would you tell me, please, which way I ought to go from here?

The Cheshire Cat: That depends a good deal on where you want to get to.

Alice: I don't much care where.

The Cheshire Cat: Then it doesn't much matter which way you go.

The first step of any journey is to pick a destination. If your destination (goal) is to be a professional fighter, your journey will be different than the guy who gets into the martial arts with the end goal of developing the skills to defend himself and his family.

One is a journey into a combat sport, where you will be training to be in top physical condition, and you will be fighting in an environment of "the known"! You will know the street. In a stressful violent encounter, you don't rise to the occasion; you sink to your level of training. If you have trained for a "known rules and factors" environment, then you will not have the conditioned reflex to respond to the "no rules and unknown factors" situation as you will need to. The tactics you train will be what you respond with when caught by surprise and have that adrenalin dump caused by the physiological effects of the fight or flight syndrome. In a combat sport you train your body to respond as a conditioned reflex according to a set of rules by which the attacker in the street will not be limited.

So if the destination (goal) of your training is the ability to protect yourself in an incident of violence, then you need to know what route will get you to that destination. There are times, even when you have looked at the map and have a good idea of the route to your destination, that you may take a wrong turn. Even a guided missile doesn't get to its target in a straight line, but by continual evaluation and course correction.

Another consideration is that this may not be a one-stop trip. You may have to stop along the line at several locations in order to get the end product you want. The chances of finding every tool you will need on your self-protection tool belt, all in one location is very slim!

EVALUATION and COURSE CORRECTION

In the martial arts journey, this is what that evaluation and course correction may look like. You find a school or class somewhere that you have heard a lot about. You run into a guy at the gas station who is wearing a shirt with the school's logo on it, so you ask him about it. It turns out that he is the instructor of the school, and he tells you just how

in advance that you will be facing only one
will know where the fight will take place,
when the fight will occur, on what kind c
under what rules you will be fighting. In m
will even know who you will be fighting. Th
that the guy training for self protection in a s
real-life encounter will never know.

The person training for self-protection h
factors to consider than those of the combat
The first consideration in self protection is that
ment you will likely be fighting in is just as dan
opponent you will be facing. No mats to protec
ground. Gravel, broken bottles, curbs, holes, un
ice, are all dangers of the street encounter. Notl
the fight contained to a safe area. If you are
balance, you aren't stopped by a cage fence or
You will have stairways, windows and traffic
with! Then there is the concern of there being
one opponent, weapons, and your possible need t
protect yourself, but your loved ones as well.

The above factors are why I do not refer
sports as "Martial" arts. Combat sports are to a n
what paintball is to a real gun fight. In paintball,
behind a car for cover and I am behind a car fifty
I may break cover, taking the chance that you c
moving target, to get a better shot at you. After all,
consequence of that decision is the sting of a pair
sport and play, with no danger of really bad conse
for bad decisions, you take chances you otherwise v
I'm not taking that chance if we are in a gunfight v
guns and real bullets!

A tactic or technique that is great in a comb;
environment may get you killed in a violent encou

awesome his classes are and how he will teach you to be a self-defense machine, so you decide to join.

When you get to the first class, they tell you to take your shoes off and train barefoot. They make you wear silly white Japanese pajamas and then begin teaching you how to use antique Okinawan farm tools (Nunchaku, Sai and Tonfa) as weapons.

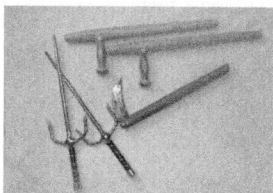

Ancient asian farm tools are not adequate modern weapons.

You begin thinking about it and ask the instructor why you have to practice barefoot when you are most likely to be wearing shoes on the street, to which the honorable sensei Replies "Its tradition".

Then you ask why you have to wear the pajamas, and he says "it is the traditional clothing for learning the method, you are learning Karate, and that's a Karate uniform! Duh!

In my younger days, Silly White Pajamas and all.
Being barefoot and in very loose clothing, designed for
the ability to kick high, seldom translates well into a
violent street encounter where you will be wearing
shoes and tighter clothing. Train as close as possible to
the way you expect to apply your skills!

5

Tony Massengill

And the uniform makes it easier for you to do the low stances and high kicks because they aren't tight like street clothes". So you think back to the fencing class you took last year .... and say to yourself "when I joined the fencing class no one made me dress like one of the Three Musketeers! How does playing dress up help my ability to defend myself? And if I need these ultra loose clothes to perform the techniques, how is that practical when I will be wearing street clothes if I have to use this stuff" Then you consider the antique Okinawan farm tools, which weren't the best choice of weapons even at the time the Okinawans had to use them, but tools of necessity, because the Okinawans were denied "Real" weapons by the occupying Japanese! So you decide it is time to correct your course, because this one seems to be a wrong turn!

Next you go out and find a Mixed-Martial-Arts gym. You think to yourself, I want to learn to fight, and this is more realistic than the "Pajama and Farm Tool Academy of Self-Defense" you just left. You look around and find big, strong, tough guys punching bags, jumping ropes, and fighting in cages. Some of them look like they eat raw meat and nails for breakfast! You think to yourself "Training with these tough guys is bound to make me good at defending myself and family"! So you join!

After you have been training a few months, you and the guys from the gym go to a sports bar to watch an MMA event. During one of the fights you see a fighter who is good .... No, you decide, he borders on great! Although the opponent gets some good shots in every now and then, this guy is tough and can take the punishment and keep moving forward! He is dominating his opponent with vicious leg kicks, and masterful ground fighting. Then something unbelievable happens. As your hero, the fighting machine is

6

punching the other guy with a great display of boxing skill, the opponent, attempting to defend one of the punches, accidentally sticks his finger in the tough guy's eye.

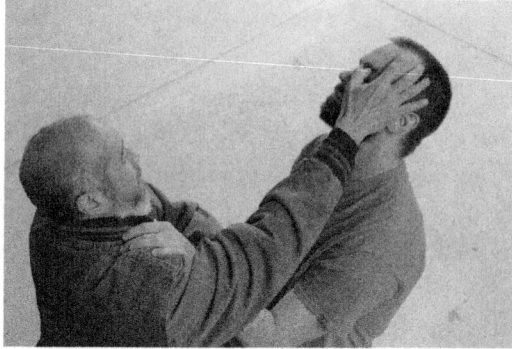

*No matter how big and tough the opponent, his eyes
are as vulnerable as those of a baby!*

To your, and everyone else's amazement, this guy, who just moments ago seemed unstoppable, dropped faster than Bill Clinton's pants in an Arkansas trailer park. This big tough dude who was walking through his opponents punches like they were marshmallows was now rolling around on the floor, holding his eye and crying like a three-year old.

At about this time, one of your fellow MMA students, the best fighter in the group, gets into an argument with someone else at the bar. As the other guy takes a swing, your classmate slides under the punch and easily takes the guy to the ground, just like you have been taught and trained to do hundreds of times at the gym. It was a textbook perfect take-down! As he mounts the downed bar thug and applies a great choke, he is kicked in the head by one of Bar Thug's friends. And before the bouncers could step in and break the fight up, one of the other good fighters from your group

7

was knocked out and cut rather badly by a beer bottle to the head. Your night ends with you accompanying your classmates to the ER.

Thus begins another evaluation. The big, tough, seemingly unstoppable fighter was taken down by a simple and accidental finger to the eye. Your friend, who applied a great take down and choke, was taken out by a second attacker. Your other classmate got dropped by a guy who hit him with a makeshift weapon. Neither scenario is addressed by your current training. The finger to the eye had a lot more effect than the heavy punches he was able to just walk through. Your gym's ground fighting game which was so dominant in the cage against just one opponent, made your classmate a sitting duck for a second attacker.

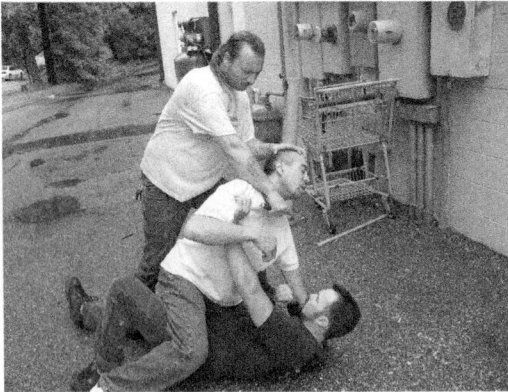

Ground and pound is a good tactic ... except for the "ground" part. In a real fight, with no rules or referee, on the ground you can't account for other attackers, or weapons!

And a beer bottle, really! That wasn't fair. But then again, this was a bar not the sporting arena. People aren't limited to the jab, cross and hook!

8

Yet another wrong turn, but not entirely wasted time. Some of the technical skills you learned will be useful to add to your self-protection tool belt. You have developed a heavy punch, and some very strong kicks, but the lack of preparedness for things outside the combat sports rules need to be addressed. It's course correction time!

To End Well ...... Start Well. Choose Your Guide Carefully

It's very important to decide on your end goal as early in your journey as possible. You should do a pre-trip assessment and know where you are headed. What skills do you believe you will need if your goal is street applicable self-protection abilities? The ability to be an effective self-defender is what I will always focus on in what I teach and write about. I have learned that no one can be all things to all people! I have my area of specialty. I am a "real world" self-protection guy. I am not a sports fighter. I was there once, but the time I spent as a police officer quickly showed me that those skills were not efficient for the street. So, out of necessity, my focus changed. That was my first conscious evaluation and course correction!

The guide you choose for your journey through the martial arts will be of great importance. It is said that Ip Man told his students "It is important to know the source of the water you drink" He used this as a metaphor for what you are being taught, and by whom. You have to give Ip Man credit, it's a great example!

The thought of your host dipping your drinking glass in the toilet and then serving it to you is a pretty powerful image. It is equally important to make sure you aren't being taught "toilet" self-defense methods by an instructor with no "real" experience!

Along the same lines, the great motivational speaker, Zig Zigler told a story of being a guest on a talk show on which another guest was an alleged relationship expert promoting her new book on how to have a great marriage. Zig stated "I knew that woman personally. She was teaching people how to have a great marriage, when she, herself, had been married so many times she had rice marks on her face" His point, although humorously made, is that you have to make sure the person teaching you has a background of knowledge and success in what they claim to teach!

In the modern commercial martial arts environment, we

see people under the age of twenty-five claiming to be masters, and teachers of multiple systems of fighting. Titles like Master and Grandmaster are thrown around like promises of "free stuff" at a Bernie Sanders rally! Bogus "Hall of Fame" awards, where promoters sell ... yes sell the awards. People pay for these awards, go to the ceremonies and then return to their schools, putting their award plaque on the wall proclaiming them a "Hall of Fame" member. Look at their backgrounds! What are they famous for? What special achievement brought them to the attention of the presenters of the award? I can answer that question. In most cases, Nothing!

Let me tell you how this scam works. Someone develops an organisation .... Let's call ours the "Brotherhood of Grandmasters Understanding Secrets" or B.O.G.U.S. for short! (Unfortunately

Brotherhood Of Grandmasters Understanding Secrets
B.O.G.U.S.
Hall Of Fame Award

Presented to
Grandmaster BillyBob Whitedude
In Recognition of his outstanding achievement of sending us a check in the amount of $500

Awarded 2/1/21

B.O.G.U.S. Grandmasters Council

these guys are never quite this obvious) Now

B.O.G.U.S. develops a Hall of Fame Award, and presents the first ones to some martial arts celebrities. Then they hire these celebrities to be presenters, guests, and seminar instructors at their annual Hall of Fame Award ceremony. After that they get a mailing list of martial arts school owners and "sell them" the opportunity to mingle and rub shoulders with the martial arts celebrities ... photo ops. and all. Then they are presented with their "Hall of Fame" award, which the unsuspecting student later sees displayed on the wall of the school and is summarily impressed! If you see one of these awards when you enter a martial arts school, don't walk.... Run away!

The flip side of the bogus awards problem is the "Weekend Instructor Certification" courses advertised in the Martial Arts trade publications. There was a magazine called "Martial Arts Professional" that I used to get when I ran a commercial martial arts school. In every issue of that magazine there were ads for KRAV MAGA Weekend Instructor Training Programs and DVD courses for XMA (Extreme Martial Arts) that could be added to your schools curriculum. I had a parent bring their teenage son, who was a black belt at another school in my area, to my school. They expressed that they wanted to change schools because the owner of the other school had bought the XMA DVD series, given them to this young man and expected him to learn from the DVDs and teach a XMA class at their school. This is just one of many examples of why choosing a guide for your martial arts journey is a 'Buyer Beware" situation for sure!

Beware of the "We teach everything" schools. If the sign in the window reads "Karate – Kung fu – Jiu Jitsu – Tae Kwon Do – Kickboxing – Tai Chi – Self-Defense – Lawn Mower Repair & Underwater Demolition" again ... Don't walk ..... RUN in the opposite direction. The reason for training in a self-protection method is to develop conditioned reflex. You can no more develop, simultaneously, the ability to "fight according to a set of rules" and "self-protection in a no rules environment" as coexisting and dependable condition reflex, than you could run in two different directions at the same time. To attempt to do so defies the law of contradiction! These two are contradictory reflexes. So if you are to be competent at either, you must choose between them.

Self-Protection in the modern era

At one time, mankind grunted at one another and fought with rocks and clubs. Through gradual advances in both language and tools, mankind graduated to cursing at one another and fighting with knives and swords. In Japan for example, the samurai carried both a long and short sword. They were great and feared warriors. But when the gun was invented, it eventually replaced the sword as the most efficient weapon. By World War II the Japanese went to war with guns, not swords. Some carried swords out of tradition, but the gun was the go-to weapon.

The weapons of the warrior have changed with the times. When the katana (Long Samurai Sword) was invented, the samurai didn't reject it and continue to fight with rocks and sticks out of respect for tradition. They upgraded to the tool which was the most efficient and best fit their needs. Wouldn't it be reasonable that the modern student of martial arts do the same?

The exclusion of weapons training is another reason I don't consider MMA a "Martial Art" but just a "Combat Sport". This is not a put-down of combat sports, just recognition of what it is, and more importantly, what it is not. Empty hand skills are of great importance in self protection, but so is the knowledge of the use of weapons if you find yourself in a situation where empty hand skills are not enough! The methods of warriors have always included the use of weapons. A weapon is the only equalizer when the enemy is measurably stronger, greater in number or if they themselves are armed. Neither of which is generally a major concern in the combat sports arena, thus these situations are not addressed in their training regime.

In modern society, while there are laws that sometimes limit what one can carry, in general, the most practical and efficient tools for self protection which can be easily carried and deployed if needed are the tactical folding knife and the handgun. To truly be interested in self protection and not have these two tools as part of your training system is a big mistake.

Modern weapons such as Handguns and folding knives should be part of training for the modern self-defender

And to ignore them but spend time practicing with archaic weapons like the Nunchaku, Tonfa, Three-Section-

Staff, Samurai Sword, Broad Sword or any other traditional "martial arts" weapon is pure lunacy! If your training does more to keep a "tradition" alive than it does to keep YOU alive, it's time for a change!

So before you choose an instructor, you owe it to yourself to do a thorough check of their background and the method they teach. Make sure that they have some practical experience. Theory is fine, but theory is not tested fact, its speculation. And you don't want your life and safety hanging on speculation! It reminds me of the Trump Impeachment sham hearings I just finished watching. The "Schiff Show" was truly a special event. What stood out to me was the statement by Democratic Illinois Rep. Mike Quigley claiming that "**hearsay** could be better than **direct evidence".** You hear this same kind of nonsense from martial arts instructors who say that although they have never been in a real self-defense situation, their theoretical methods could be better than actual direct experience. Both of the above statements are the nonsensical ravings of a lunatic mind!

So choose your desired goal, your guides and carefully plan your path. Make periodic evaluations to make sure you are still on the path to your intended destination and make course corrections as necessary.

May GOD Bless your travels, and see you through to your destination!

Chapter 2

The Only Thing Constant is Change

Wing Chun changes with every hand it passes through. In the movie "Ip Man - The Legend Begins" My SiGung (my teachers teacher) Ip Chun, Eldest son of Grandmaster Ip Man, plays the part of Leung Bik, one of Ip Man's teachers. In a scene where Ip Man first meets Leung Bik, who eventually became his final instructor, and before he knows that the man he has met is the son of his Sigung, Ip Man questions the authenticity of Leung Bik's Wing Chun. Leung Bik responds that "the only one, who has ever done AUTHENTIC Wing Chun, was the founder of the system, Ng Mui". This is a very enlightening scene.

Everyone who teaches a system, in this case, Wing Chun, in some way, intentionally or unintentionally, leaves their personal mark on the system. Today we speak of Wong Shun Leung Ving Tsun / Wing Chun, William Cheung Wing Chun, Leung Ting Wing Tsun,..... all methods drawing their foundation from the Wing Chun taught by Ip Man. But it has changed.... and this is not necessarily a bad thing. It is a necessity for the survival of the system as a viable method of self-protection as times change.

If you examine many of the principles and theories upon which Bruce Lee built his martial arts system, Jeet Kune Do, you will find them to be an expansion of the principles you see taught by Wong Shun Leung, who was one of the primary people responsible for Bruce Lee's martial education.

Years ago I recommended a book to one of my students, Jason Korol, who is both a Wing Chun instructor under my organisation as well as being a long time JKD instructor.

The book was "Beyond the pointing finger - The Combat Philosophy of Wong S

This is a great book and should be in every Wing Chun students collection

hun Leung", authored by David Peterson, a book about Ip Man's student, Wong Shun Leung and his methods (Wong was the assistant instructor in Ip Man's school when Bruce Lee was a student there) Jason stated, after reading the book, that it was the best JKD book he had ever read. He explained that what he read of Wong Shun Leung's ideas, were exactly what had been taught to him as JKD methodology.

Jason has written a very good book, "Jeet Kune Do - Pure and Simple" , which points out that Bruce Lee, according to Ted Wong, one of Bruce Lee's long time original students, researched "old school" western boxing to find the kinship of the method to the Wing Chun he had studied.... This is the boxing method to which Wong Shun Leung would have been exposed.

He utilised the methods which fit the Wing Chun

17

structure in which he already had a strong foundation, and added those which fit his needs to fill the gaps left by his incomplete training under Ip Man and Wong Shun Leung.

Bruce's research led to methods taught by legendary Western boxers like Jim Driscol and Jack Dempsey. These boxers utilised methods which were amazingly similar to those of Wing Chun, as taught to Lee. To understand this, we must understand that Wong Shun Leung had studied Western Boxing prior to his involvement with Wing Chun. Wong made an instructional video in the early 80's called "The Science of In-Fighting" that can be found on YouTube. In it, Wong demonstrates his footwork. When compared with many other Wing Chun instructors, his footwork was much more mobile, much more akin to Western Boxing, than the footwork demonstrated by many of his classmates under Ip Man. I believe it was Wong's innovations in his use of mobility that set his version of Wing Chun and thus Bruce Lee's foundation, apart from other Wing Chun methods! It is one of the reasons that I (the author) took the time, and expense of researching and cross-training in the Wong Shun Leung method, after being awarded a Master Instructor level certification in the Ip FAMILY method. I concluded Wong didn't add to the Wing Chun system, as taught to him by Ip Man, but just utilised the tools in a different way, as he understood them, with his understanding of Western Boxing!

It was these methods that expanded Bruce Lee's understanding of fighting, as taught to him, primarily by the most experienced fighter of the Ip Man Wing Chun clan ..... Wong Shun Leung.

This leads me to believe two things .... Bruce Lee was

the first to begin the spread of what today is known as Wong Shun Leung Ving Tsun, which eventually for Bruce Lee, became Jeet Kune Do. Which leads to my second conclusion, Jeet Kune Do was simply Bruce Lee's Wing Chun. There are those who may disagree with me, but that's ok, ... we can't all be right... :-)

Let's explore some of these similarities. Old school boxing was much more of a flat footed slug fest than what is seen in modern Western Boxing.

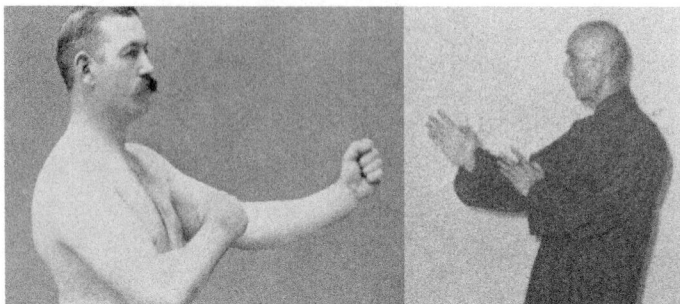

John L. Sullivan's and Ip Man's fighting guard position are just one example of the kinship between "old school" western boxing and Wing Chun

The basic guard was very similar. The close (Clinch) range methodology such as footwork and the control of the other fighters hands were alike as well.

Although it was much more flat footed than in today's more movement oriented, stick and move, methodology, there was still an "outside game".... a distance fighting method which was not emphasised as much in the traditional Wing Chun method as taught by Ip Man.

Wong Shun Leung, as pointed out earlier, seemed to utilise the footwork in a way that was much more mobile than what is seen in many other lineages that descend from Ip Man. I believe the reason for this was from his previous background in Western Boxing combined with his "practical fight experience" which gave him an understanding of Wing Chun footwork that others didn't see! Unlike many of his classmates, Wong actually fought with Wing Chun in challenge matches. One of the tools he brought with him from

Western Boxing was the understanding of footwork and strategic positioning (movement). This experience taught him the need for more mobility outside of bridge contact (the clinch in Western Boxing), and how to more effectively utilise tactical footwork to gain bridge control of his opponents.

Footwork is nothing more than a transportation system. Like all transportation systems, they are limited by the environment in which they are used. A boat, for example, is an excellent mode of transportation, on the water .... but, it is useless on the highway! The car, while great on the highway, is equally useless in the water! Each has its optimal environment of usefulness. Footwork has exactly the same limitations.

Dancing and slick movement seen at a distance in Western Boxing, is pretty much useless once engaged in a clinch with the opponent. In a clinch, flat footed, rooted footwork is preferred in order to maintain balance and the ability to defend and attack efficiently, the same would be true on uneven ground or an environment with obstacles, such as curbs or staircases!

Conversely, being flat footed in the middle of the ring when facing a mobile opponent will likely result in being "picked apart" by an opponent who can slide in, hit and slide out before you can react.

Each has its place. The problem, as I see it, is the stubborn blindness of Wing Chun people in attempting to utilise a rooted footwork, designed for bridge contact (clinch), at a distance where mobility is not only preferred, but desperately needed.

Now I believe that both Master Wong and Bruce Lee were focused quite a bit on testing their method against other fighters. This is not necessarily a bad thing, but in doing so in a primarily friendly environment, meaning not while defending oneself from a sudden violent attack, but against an opponent in a mutually agreed upon contest, changes the method of use, and intent of application.

The importance of this distance oriented footwork is greatly reduced when looking at Wing chun purely as a self-protection system to be used in a "real" sudden violent encounter and not a more "sport oriented" contest. I am not suggesting that it is not useful and important to develop, but suggesting that in a contest, we find more need to close the distance with the opponent. In a "real-world" street encounter, it is better to escape, or pick something up to use as a weapon of defense, if there is that much distance between the thug and yourself. Closing that distance is generally the bad guys burden, not yours in a real fight!

That point being made, I still believe that developing more mobile footwork in addition to the close range foot-work works to your advantage. While there is limited need to close from a distance, empty handed, to the opponent in the street, that doesn't mean that you will never have a situa-tion that requires that ability, so why limit yourself to just close range footwork, when you can develop more mobile footwork as well?

Wong Shun Leung and his protégée Bruce Lee both recognised this! And this is what makes their methodology different from many other Wing Chun linages. I believe we can all learn a valuable lesson by standing on the shoulders of these giants!

Think about it, why on earth would someone insist on reinventing the combustion engine every year they come out with a new model of car?

We build the future on the shoulders of the giants of the past! But, we need to examine what has been passed to us, evaluate the lessons, keep what fits in our modern world, and discard what doesn't. We owe a great debt of gratitude to the Wing Chun masters of the past ...... but we are not slaves to their understanding of the fighting arts! What is needed for practical application changes with each and every generation! So, thank you oh ancient ones, you did your part...... but, relax .... We've got it from here!

Chapter 3

Systematic Self-Protection Training

In order to teach any skill, and stay consistent with the instruction, the skill must be taught in a systematic way. My instructional approach is to divide physical skills into the following five categories.

Those five categories are:
1. Form
2. Footwork
3. Offensive Tool Development
4. Training Drills
5. Application

In some training, there will be overlap between each of these five, but understanding these categories will help the student grasp each area of importance.

The five category approach to systematic training will be pretty much the same whether training from an empty hand platform, blade platform, impact weapons platform or firearms platform. While each has its own set of K.S.A's (Knowledge, Skills and Abilities), these five categories will be used in the development of all of them!

Form

Most of the time, when we hear the term form or training set, we think in terms of traditional martial arts. The Japanese call it Kata. It's called Poomse or Hyung to the Koreans and Taolu or Kuen to the Chinese.

Master Edmund Fong performing the third form of Wing Chun, Biu Gee, at the Ip Man Museum in Foshan, China.

In actuality, a form can be any set of movements, done sequentially, that comprise a mechanical skill. So yes, a form can be a traditional training set, such as Wing Chun's Siu Lim Tao, but it can also be a Western Boxing training pattern, or combination such as Jab, Cross, Hook, or it can be the movements that comprise the skill of drawing a handgun from a concealed position taking a proper grip and getting target acquisition. There are even sequential training sets "forms" in tactical pistol-craft for combat and tactical reloads! Forms teach proper mechanical skills, structure, angle and alignment of the technique being trained. Forms are a great method of solo training and can be developed to gain a level of mastery with just about any skill.

Footwork

Footwork is the foundation upon which all else is built. Proper footwork will be chosen depending upon the needs of the situation you find yourself at any particular time. Footwork, is nothing more, nor anything less than transportation. And your chosen mode of transportation will depend on the reason and need for the transportation and the environment in which it will be employed.

In your everyday life you will choose different transportation for differing needs. If you need to move a refrigerator, a compact car is probably not your best choice! If you are traveling down a wooded path, then a Corvette would be a poor choice. If you are racing against a sports car, then a moving van would not be an efficient choice ..... You get the idea!

In fighting, footwork can be as simple as "move from point A to point B, hit the guy and don't fall down in the process". Footwork can also be as complicated as the use of the legs and hips in conjunction with the step and turn to develop dynamic power. We will attempt to help you understand the path to navigate from one extreme to the other. Much like life, you crawl before you walk and walk before you run... but then, that's just transportation, isn't it!

Close range footwork and kicking will be of great importance in your ability to defend yourself in a violent encounter

The same is true of footwork. Empty handed confrontations at extreme close range, or in a confined space , such as an elevator, will require a different set of footwork needs than those of a longer range, less confined confrontation. Deploying a knife against an armed assailant will usually require different footwork needs than those of empty hand fighting. Firing a pistol while moving will require a different footwork, in order to move and hit a target, than the footwork used in other fighting needs.

The path to mastery of footwork is a time consuming activity, but the rewards for that time will be great! Putting your weapon (Empty hand, blade or gun) on top of a strong transportation and delivery system will make you formidable! Put that same weapon on top of weak footwork and the result is disastrous. Picture a strong knight jousting, mounted on a great horse. Then picture that same knight on an old worn out donkey, and you will understand the importance of your weapons delivery system!

Offensive Tool Development

Offensive Tool development describes the training, understanding and use of hands, elbows, knees, feet, in extreme cases teeth and head butts, as well as blade and firearm.

One of my senior students, Andrew Tate, does some tool training.

Empty hand tool development covers elements such as, how to hit, power development and proper striking angles . Non-empty hand tool development includes such skills as knife or handgun grip, cutting angles and proper trigger control.

Empty hand tool development isn't about "iron palm" training or beating your hands to a bloody pulp in an attempt to "toughen" them. There are actually people out there in the martial arts world who will tell you that their "Iron Palm" training leaves them afraid of picking up their baby or touching their spouse, because the training has made them so dangerous! Seriously ... They act as if they are afraid they may tear a butt cheek off if they pat their significant other on the back side!! Leave that Kung Fu fantasy crap to the old Shaw Brothers classics, it has no place in the real world!

Over the many years I have been involved in the martial arts I have seen some people do some really stupid and self-destructive things in the name of "toughening" the hands, and legs. Trust me when I tell you the following, at the age of sixty, and having trained in the martial arts since the age of five, I have learned one very valuable training lesson. All of the injuries you sustain in training will haunt you when you get old! Think long and hard on this point before embarking on some stupid "traditional" training regime, like Iron Palm training!, or other such nonsense.

We must think about what we will actually be utilising these tools (hands and legs) to do. If we have to use our hands, for example, to protect ourselves in a violent attack, we will be using them against another mortal human being. We have soft vulnerable targets to exploit. Just how "tough" do you think your hands have to be to stick a thumb in the violent predators eye?

Training Drills

Training drills come in both partner and solo varieties. In Wing Chun for example, there is an entire training set utilising the wooden dummy as a training tool.

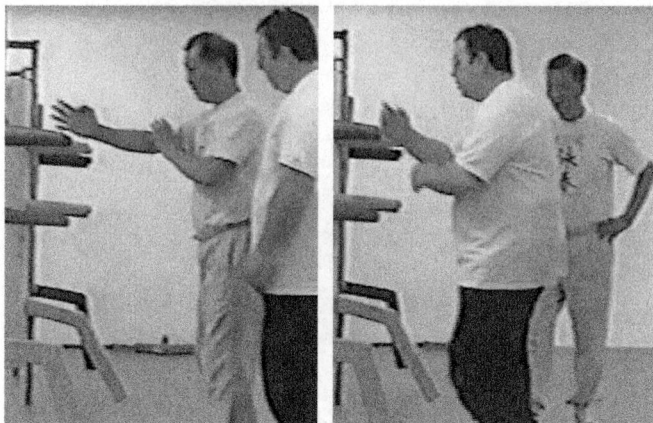

Working with Ip Ching for the first time back in 1996

*Training the wooden dummy under the watchful eyes
of Samuel Kwok and Grandmaster Ip Ching, at Ip
Ching's home in Hong Kong*

There are also different solo drills utilising the wooden dummy, punching bags and other such equipment.

In addition to these solo drills are numerous partner assisted training drills that develop the student's skills into conditioned reflex.

Drills are usually utilised to develop specific mechanical skills as well as general attributes, such as speed, balance and distance control, which will be "plugged in" to your fighting ability. Wing Chun is a method that is rich in many such training drills.

In knife training, training knives are used to get as close to realistic as possible.

In the use of the blade, training drills include the training of cutting on such training apparatus as the battle post, as well as partner drills utilising training knives. In tactical firearms training we utilise computer shot-recording software along with LASR laser training guns for shot accuracy and speed while developing the skill of moving and firing or drawing and firing for solo training.

LASR training guns, Airsoft training guns, targets, and force-on-force live action training are all used in tactical firearms training.

We use an Airsoft training platform for "live action" drills with a training partner to develop skills such as weapons retention and moving from empty hand to weapon deployment against an attacker.

People often mistake training drills for application of the system in actual self-protection. To understand what I mean by this, let's examine the following. The Wing Chun system consists of three empty hand forms, Siu Lim Tao, Chum Kiu and Biu Jee. One set of movements on the Wooden Dummy training apparatus, and two weapon sets, the pole or Luk Deem Boon Kwun and the knives or Baat Jam Dao. That is the SYSTEM. Training drills or methods are the ways the tools of the system are developed. The system is the axe. Sharpening the axe isn't the same as using the axe ... but it is a necessary component in the use of the axe!

The system is the skeletal structure. The training methods are the flesh! While the system itself should stay consistent from one instructor to the next, the methods of training and developing the system for application are open to change and invention, limited only by the imagination of the trainee!

Application

All of the first four categories are meant to develop the tools, knowledge, skills and abilities, with the focus on the fifth, actual application.

Me with my first Wing Chun teacher, Duncan (Shiu Hung) Leung

I began training in Wing Chun in 1979. My first teacher, Duncan (Shiu Hung) Leung, always said that the ultimate goal of any martial art is its use in a fight, and if what you are practicing doesn't lead to that end goal, then you are wasting your training time. I have always felt that this was some of the best advice I have ever been given in my many years of martial arts training.

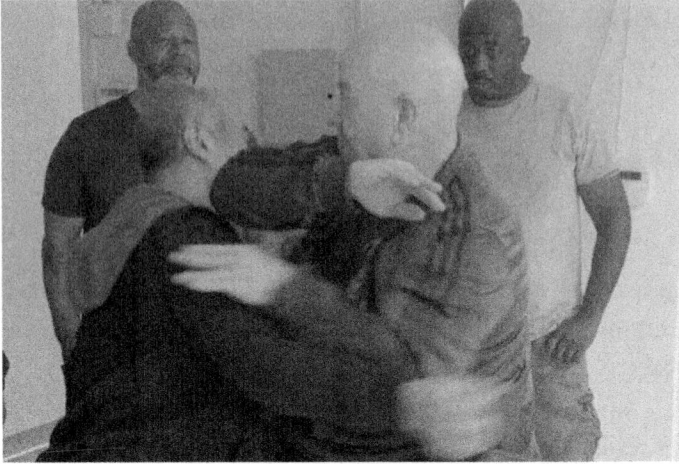

While different elements may be worked in training drills separately, all must be combined in order to apply your skills in a dynamic setting. As Sifu Leung advised me when I began Wing Chun. "the ultimate goal of any martial art is its use in a fight, and if what you are practicing doesn't lead to that end goal, then you are wasting your training time".

The unfortunate truth is, that in many traditional martial arts schools, training in practical application and preparation for use in a real world violent encounter, as opposed to sporting application, are as hard to find as a coherent sentence in a Joe Biden speech!

This was one of the things that drew me to Wing Chun in the first place! I had been training in the martial arts since the age of five. I trained in a number of disciplines, including Judo, Shotokan Karate and Praying Mantis Kung Fu. I had earned black belt rank Tae Kwon Do, Kenpo, and Kajukenbo. The one thing that all of these methods had in common was that they had training forms (kata) and training drills or two-person training sets that were not in line with how people actually fought.

I remember a conversation with a karate instructor from

my local area, who I understand is a very talented fighter. He had seen a flier that I had used when I ran a commercial school several years earlier. I seemed to bother him a lot, He had actually kept a copy of the flier in his office!

The flier had a photo of a casket on the front, with a framed black belt certificate sitting on top and a black belt draped over the top of it. The words "Don't bet your life on Sport Karate of Tae Kwon Do" in bold print over the top.

Bold, well yea ... but then again, subtlety has never been one of my superpowers!

This instructor raised an objection to me about the statement. He asked me "are you saying I can't fight"? To which I replied "Not at all, I understand you are a quite talented fighter. My premise is that you don't fight with karate ..... You kick box! You don't use traditional down blocks, outside blocks and inside blocks like the ones you teach your students in the traditional forms. You cover, parry, bob and weave like a boxer. You don't use front stances, horse stances and back stances like you teach in your forms. You use a boxer's footwork. You shuffle step, advance angle step and pivot like a western boxer. You don't use Corkscrew punched like those in your forms, you use jab, cross, hook." So my contention was that while he is a very good fighter, he didn't fight with "traditional karate". I remember leaving him pretty much speechless!

But as I said, this is one of the things that initially drew me to Wing Chun. The forms are not set up like some kind of fight scene against an invisible opponent, using mechanical, stiff, impractical movements as many of the traditional forms of karate, kung fu and taekwondo are. They are more of a training set of individual techniques, set up in a pattern for learning, not in an order for specific "this follows that " type of application. It is much more like the English alphabet song, where the letters are not in an order that would dictate use in forming words.

When I watched Wing Chun people apply their method in sparring, I could see that the techniques actually came from what they were practicing in the drills and forms, not divorced from the hours of training done in class like I had found in the karate training from my past! As a matter of fact, we used to jokingly say that the inventors of Wing Chun were very sneaky! They hid the fighting techniques in the forms, because they knew Karate practitioners would never think to look there!

I know that there are some readers who may see it as disrespectful to say these things about karate, and that as a teacher of Wing Chun I shouldn't say these things. But I dedicated the time to earning Black Belt ranks in two karate systems before beginning my training in Wing Chun, so I think I have earned the right to have these opinions!

Practical application should be the ultimate focus of any training to which you dedicate your time. Training should either develop attributes which have a direct impact on your fighting ability, such as speed, timing, distance control and accuracy, or on your fighting ability itself. If the end goal is not directly improving your ability to fight, your training time is being wasted!

Method Overlap

While methods and techniques will differ from one "system" to another, the foundational principles and tactics of deploying those techniques are pretty much universal. For this reason, I will often use the example of weapons (Blade and Firearm) to emphasise empty hand training and application, and empty hand examples to help the student understand weapons use. I do this because my background includes both, and I have found that in the end, in real world application, basic principles of use overlap quite a bit between empty hand and weapons use!

Chapter 4

Building the Weapon

The first training set in the Wing Chun system is called Siu Lim Tao (Little Idea). This form will be the foundation of all that will follow in Wing Chun. This training form is very different from the forms of many other karate and kung fu systems. Other systems have forms called Katas or Kuen, that are set up like a choreographed fight scene against imaginary opponents. That is not the case with the Siu Lim Tao form.

Ip Ching watches as his father performs the Siu Lim Tao form. This photo always reminds me of what a rare opportunity Ip Ching had, sharing a home with his father.

The Siu Lim Tao form is much more akin to the English alphabet than a prearranged imaginary fighting set. When we begin learning the alphabet, we learn the "alphabet song" which teaches us all twenty-six letters. The song helps us commit the letters of the alphabet to memory. We then begin to learn to write the letters. We begin with the proper shape and structure of each letter, and how to write it, first as a block letter, then the proper cursive structure of the letter. No two people will write the letters exactly the same. We will all develop our own distinctive handwriting, but it will still be recognised as the same alphabet. We are taught the sound of the letter, and learn how to combine various letters to form words. We learn the definitions of the words, and eventually learn to put words together to express thought. And eventually we learn to communicate in speech and writing.

Siu Lim Tao, being the foundation of Wing Chun, is learned and used in much the same way. The techniques of Siu Lim Tao are taught in a specific sequence, just as in the "alphabet song". The Wing Chun form, like the "alphabet song" has a sequence that is meant to help us commit the movements to memory, but not a sequence which will dictate the order or method of use.

In the English alphabet we are taught that the letters Q, R, and S are in sequence. But "Qrs" is not a word in the English language, nor is it a functional use of those letters. But you can take any of those letters, and combine them with other letters elsewhere in the alphabet and form a functional word. The techniques of the Siu Lim Tao are combined in the same way.

The order of the movements in the form has nothing to do with the way the movements will be applied. So the student must not look at the form as some kind of pre-arranged sequence that is meant to be applied in order. Each technique must be studied as an individual component, apart from the technique that precedes or follows it. Each individual technique should be studied in order to understand its structure, angle, energy and relationship to certain reference points on one's own body, which will be explained elsewhere in this book, in the section on principle and theory of Wing Chun.

It's all about Me

In learning the first Wing Chun form, no thought is given to an opponent. This form teaches "self-reference" or how the movements relate to our own body. This builds the structure that will become your weapon.

*The Siu Lim Tao is the foundation of the Wing Chun
students understanding of how offensive and defensive
tools are best supported by their natural structure.*

It is not until that weapon is built and fully functional that we will begin to think in terms of its use against an opponent.

According to Grandmaster Ip Chun, eldest son of Grandmaster Ip Man, "The Siu Lim Tao is divided into three distinct sections, each with a purpose. The first section is for building the correct energy. Concentration is on the fingertips, thumb, wrist, and elbow. The second section is about using the energy, focusing it to the end, the last six inches, which is the way Wing Chun uses power. In Wing Chun we learn that the use of Power (Gung Lik) in a technique is reserved for the very end of the technique, and should last for a very short time. The power is very explosive and is born out of relaxation. We relax, explode, and relax again. The third section of Siu Lim Tao is about training the use of this power and learning the "relax, explode, relax" timing for each technique.

Ip Man's Modification

The Siu Lim Tao form is said to have gone through a modification process under Grandmaster Ip Man. As the story goes, one of Ip Man's students, another great figure in Wing Chun, the legendary fighter, Wong Shun Leung, had been involved in a fight, which he won, but had gotten hit by a low line punch for which his defensive technique didn't work.

As the story is told, he came to Ip Man and explained how his opponent had delivered the punch and that the technique, from the Siu Lim Tao form, designed to defend low line punches had not covered low enough to stop this particular punching method. The defensive technique was Jaum Sao (Sinking Hand), a movement that covers the low area of the upper body with the sinking elbow. While this is an effective method against someone standing erect and delivering a punch to the stomach area, it was not an effective movement against someone who dropped into a low horse stance and delivered a straight punch as opposed to an angled punch from an up-right position.

Upon discussing this with Wong, and assessing the deficiencies of defending the lower section of the upper body against such attacks, Ip Man modified the third section of the form to include the Gaun Sao (Sweeping Low Block) in place of the Jaum Sao, which was already taught in the second section of the form, and so he felt would not be missed in the third section.

This new method of performing the Siu Lim Tao became the standard for the Ip Man system. His student Wong Shun Leung adopted the change, but maintained the original method as well. So his form has the original Jaum Sao section, followed by the modified Gaun Sao section. I myself teach both the traditional Ip Man method as well as the modified method to my students, as I believe both to have merit.

Not for Demonstration

Wing Chun is known for its practical, efficient, combat effectiveness, not for being pretty to watch. For this reason, the reader will find that the Siu Lim Tao form, like the other training sets in Wing Chun, is not a spectacular, exciting, performance based form, suitable for demonstrations or competition. The form has just one purpose, and that is to make the practitioner a better self-defender.

My student Jason Korol has written a great book on Wing Chun that I highly recommend, called "Wing Chun for the Modern Warrior" which can be found on Amazon.com.

In it, he describes Wing Chun as the Glock of martial arts. Unlike the sleek, smooth lines of other firearms, the Glock is very square and blocky. It's not what most people would consider a "pretty" gun, but to us "Glock people" we find the beauty of the Glock in its simplicity and dependability! I think that comparison is brilliant! To be honest,

I'm a little pissed off that he came up with that comparison before I did, but I guess I will have to live with it! :-) But seriously, it is a great comparison.

The goal of Wing Chun is not to be pretty during the fight, but to be efficient. You can worry about being pretty after the fight! There you go Jason, beat that one!

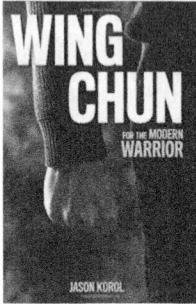

A great book that I highly recommend! And not just because there are photos of me in it, but that is certainly a plus! :-)

The Siu Lim Tao form has no footwork after the initial set up of the basic training horse known as (Yee Jee Keem Yeung Ma) or more simply, (Siu Lim Tao Ma) First Form Stance. Once that stance is assumed by the practitioner, there is no further footwork in this training form. This allows the practitioner to concentrate on the hand movements while at the same time training the horse stance which is held throughout the form, strengthening the legs and teaching the student to have a proper base foundation.

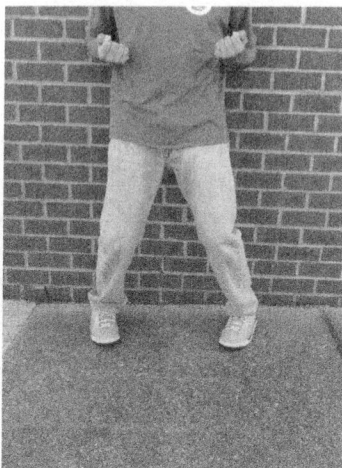

The Siu Lim Tao horse stance, Called Yee Jee Keem Yeung Ma, which translated means "character two goat restraining stance. We simply call it the Siu Lim Tao Ma.

This stance will be the basis for all footwork in the system, and helps the student to learn to relax and develop the proper rooted posture which will be the structural foundation which supports the defensive and offensive hand movements of the system. But the practitioner needs to keep in mind that this is a "training" stance, not a "fighting" stance.

The subject of footwork sets Wing Chun apart from most other fighting methods of the orient. As a matter of fact, Wing Chun seems to be much more related to Western Boxing than other Kung Fu systems in this aspect. Most martial art systems speak of differing stances, such as Horse Stance, Cat Stance, Dragon Stance, Cross Stance etc. And practice such things as "stance holding" standing in a low stance for long periods of time. Wing Chun, on the other hand, like Western Boxing, focuses on footwork in a dynamic fighting environment rather than in static balance in a stationary position.

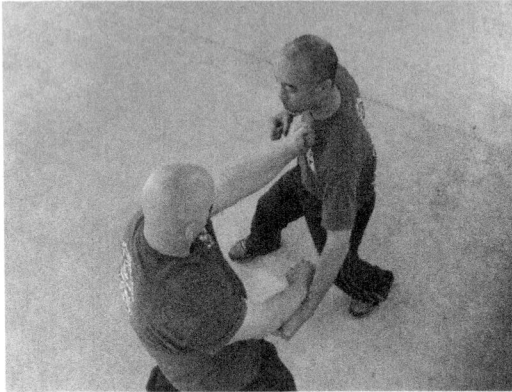

The eventual combination of the hand techniques learned in Wing Chun's first form, and the footwork learned in supplemental training as well as in the second and third training forms and wooden dummy set, will form the foundational structure of the fighting method used by the Wing Chun practitioner.

I cover this material in-depth in our Videos, Seminars and Distance Learning program. For information you can visit our web site: www. EfficientWarrior.com

Chapter 5

The Foundation Principles

Along with the individual defensive and offensive techniques, the foundation principles of the Wing Chun Kung Fu system are found within the first form. The Siu Lim Tao is like a tool belt that holds all of your fighting tools. Within this form are the basic theories, and principles that power this highly effective method of combat. As mentioned in the last chapter, the form is basically an alphabet of motion, which along with the principles teaches the structure of the fighting system. Much like the English alphabet, the more you understand about the principles of use, the more effective the tools will be.

As you will see as you read this book, Tom Clancy had a much greater understanding of the English alphabet, and its principles of use, than I do, so he could do much more with it. Wing Chun works in much the same way. The more you understand about the principles, the more you will be able to do with the tools. This allows for a great deal of personal expression. If only I had the understanding, imagination and mastery of English that Mr. Clancy did, I would be a lot more secure in my economic future ..... but you get the idea!

Wing Chun's First Form – The Nucleus

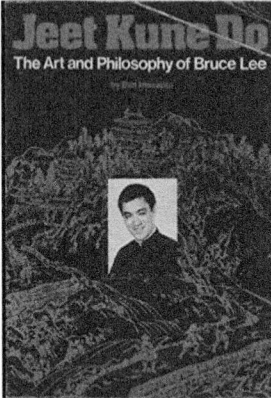

Those readers who are exploring Wing Chun because of their involvement in Bruce Lee's off-shoot of the system, Jeet Kune Do, may find it interesting that Lee's student, Dan Inosanto, in his book "Jeet Kune Do – the Art and Philosophy of Bruce Lee" called Wing Chun the Nucleus of Jeet Kune Do!

If this is true, which I believe it to be, then Wing Chun's first form should be of extreme interest to you, because Siu Lim Tao is the nucleus of Wing Chun!

The first Wing Chun form is usually taught in three sections. In the beginning, the most important thing for the student to concentrate on is learning the proper pattern of the form. Once that is learned, then the student can correct the angles and placement of the movements in the form. Grandmaster Ip Ching, taught specific reference points for each of the hand positions in the Siu Lim Tao. Many instructors teach the form haphazardly, with very few real details. Mastery is in the details. Grandmaster Ip Ching said that "in training with the proper reference points the student will develop the "Proper Standard" for performing the Siu Lim Tao. With the proper standard of doing the form, the student will avoid developing bad habits in the use of Wing Chun".

I had been a student of Wing Chun for over twenty years, and had learned the entire system, under several different instructors, prior to having the opportunity to train with Ip Ching for the first time in 1996.

Between 1996 and 2007 I was blessed to have had several extended occasions to train privately with Ip Ching, who covered the entire system, in great detail with me. Before my time with Ip Ching, I thought I knew Wing Chun. It was that time with Ip Ching as well as the years with Sifu, Samuel Kwok, and time with Sifu Edmund Fong, a top student of Ip Ching that led to an awakening of my understanding of this magnificent system.

In Grandmaster Ip Ching's method of teaching the Siu Lim Tao, the upper body is divided into three levels, upper, middle and lower. The practitioners Centerline bisect each of these levels, I will explain more on that in the next section!

Each of the hand positions will have a proper placement within one of the six areas. This kind of precise training of the form gives the student a much more detailed and specific way of training the form, and will assist in the development of "body memory" in the application of each technique.

It's much like when you get in your car and insert your key in the ignition in order to start the car. When was the last time you had to stop and actually look at the key slot in order to insert the key and start the car? I bet you can't think of the last time! That's because you have built body memory for just the right height and distance from your body to insert the key. Body memory is a key factor in being able to depend on your training method being there for you when you need it!

Centerline Theory:

In order to better understand the body's best structural positions and, and how to protect vital targets, Wing Chun teaches the student to think of the body as being bisected into two equal halves by an imaginary line referred to as the Centerline. This is not only a line that runs vertically down the middle of the body from the top of the head to the floor, but it is also seen as a plane that extends directly from the middle of the body out to the length of the arms. When the student moves, so too does this Centerline. Wherever the center of the chest faces, the Centerline plane will be directly in front.

If you imagine that you have been shot in the chest with an arrow, that arrow will extend in the direction of wherever your body faces. This gives the student a permanent natural reference point for hand placement in defense and attack. The training done in the beginning phase of Wing Chun, through proper practice of the first empty hand boxing form, Siu Lim Tao, is what produces that body memory I referenced earlier.

Teaching the body Kung Fu

This "body memory" is often referred to as "teaching the body Kung Fu". It works in much the same way as in any other physical exercise in our lives. For example, when you drive someone else's car, you often find yourself reaching "out of habit" for the position of the gearshift in your own car. This is due to the body seeking what it has been taught to do. You need to shift gears, so the mind sends the signal to do so. The limbs respond to the order by reaching for the position of the gearshift. That position has been burned into the body's "Memory" through the repetition of reaching for the gear shift in your own car so many times. This is the same way the limbs will be trained to seek the centerline when the mind sends the signal to protect the body from attack.

The centerline is important in defense because most of the body's vital points run along this line, or within a few inches of it. The eyes, throat, solar plexus, and groin all lie on this line. Protection of these vital areas is of utmost importance to the student's ability to protect themselves in a violent encounter. It is also important to remember that the opponent will be just as weak in these areas as you are, so it will be in your best interest to focus your attacks to the opponents Centerline if possible.

. . .

Theory of facing

In order to take full advantage of protecting their Centerline, the Wing Chun student will be taught the theory of facing. This method teaches that the Wing Chun exponent should always face the opponent squarely. This will keep the shoulders square to the opponent, and allow the greatest freedom of movement, in using the centerline to its fullest structural advantage and allowing the best protection of ones own vital areas. If the Wing Chun exponent were to place one side forward, such as in a western boxing position, this would limit movement to the rear side in both defense and attack. The goal is to face the opponent squarely while preventing the opponent from being able to do the same to you. The structure of the Wing Chun system, in the theory of facing is based on the triangle.

Triangle structure

The triangle is one of the most sound structural shapes. In Wing Chun the triangle is used to a high degree of advantage.

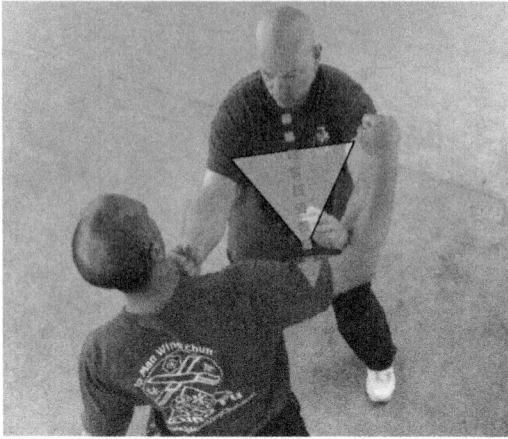

The triangle is formed by using the shoulders as the base of the triangle, with the centerline plane as the point, directly in front of the body.

When the Wing Chun exponent faces an opponent squarely, the triangle is formed by using the shoulders as the base of the triangle, with the centerline plane as the point, directly in front of the body. The point of the triangle is used as the reference point for hand placement for proper body structure of the defensive hand tools of Wing Chun.

By understanding the proper hand position in the placement of the blocking hand, the body's natural structure can be used instead of unnecessary muscular strength. This makes Wing Chun work by way of "method, not muscle". A properly placed defending hand can be used as a wedge in order to gain entry into the opponent's defense. This method combined with the ability to pivot the footwork will enable the Wing Chun exponent to effectively counter a strong aggressive attack, even from a stronger opponent.

. . .

The Stance

The entire Siu Lim Tao is performed from one stationary stance. That stance is the "Yee" Jee Keem Yeung Ma (Character "Two" adduction stance). This is a descriptive name that is meant to give an understanding of what the stance looks and feels like. In English, when I say Character "Two", in your mind's eye, you see "2". But the Chinese see

This Character is used to describe the position of the toes, in relation to the heels. The stance is a Pigeon-toed position with the toes closer together than the heels. The Character Two also describes the knees in relation to the ankles. The knees are closer than the ankles. The word adduction means to "bring towards". This describes the action of the knees, which press inward towards each other. This is the stabilising force of this stance. (Siu Lim Tao Ma)

Shifting or rooting of the horse

The shifting or rooting of the horse is the transition from the Siu Lim Tao Ma, which is a 50/50 weighted stance, to the second form variation, Chum Kiu Ma, which positions the entire balance on one leg. It is this shift that allows the Wing Chun exponent to borrow the incoming force of an attack, and return to force to the opponent with interest. Chum Kiu Ma is the fighting footwork of Wing Chun. It is not as much a stance as it is footwork. Chum Kiu Ma is a dynamic position that has its use in transition. Through the shifting from one side weighted position to the other, the Wing Chun student creates the body energy that drives his or her Wing Chun.

Once again, the triangle is a major key in understanding the stability and structure of the rooted horse. In the transition from Siu Lim Tao Ma to Chum Kiu Ma, there is a relationship between the Knee of the leg that will become load bearing, and the toe of the opposite foot. It will be as if the knee is attached to the toe by an invisible rod. As the weight shifts to the load bearing leg, the knee of that leg will sink towards the floor. The toe of the opposite foot will be pushed outward, the same distance as the opposite knee sinks.

*there is a relationship between the Knee of the leg that
will become load bearing, and the toe of the opposite
foot. It will be as if the knee is attached to the toe by an
invisible rod. As the weight shifts to the load bearing
leg, the knee of that leg will sink towards the floor. The
toe of the opposite foot will be pushed outward, the
same distance as the opposite knee sinks. It should be
as if the knee pushes the toe to the outside.*

It should be as if the knee pushes the toe to the outside. It is important that the toe does not travel any further than the distance that the knee moves. If the toe travels further than the knee, then the position will become unstable.

The front to back stability will also be dependent on the triangle structure. The upper body should be in proper alignment, and should not lean forward or backward. This is a balanced footwork, with the balance on the load bearing leg, and the non load bearing leg always available to kick, without the need to shift the body weight. (Photo of front to back stability, triangle. Front leg able to kick.)

Pivoting, the ability to borrow force

When an opponent applies force, the Wing Chun student trains not to oppose the force, but to pivot and borrow the force and return it to the opponent. This ability to use the opponent's force is one of the factors that make Wing Chun effective. It may help to understand this principle if we view the body as a cylinder. When force is placed on the cylinder, the cylinder will move (rotate) in the direction of the force. The opposite side of the cylinder will move at the same pace in the opposite direction of the applied force. This falls in line with Newton's law that states that for every action, there is an equal but opposite reaction. So as one side is forced back, the other side is driven forward at the same pace. The Wing Chun exponent uses this action to dissipate the force of an attack, while launching an effective counter-offensive strike, by borrowing the opponent's force. With the Wing Chun practitioners energy added to that borrowed from the opponent, this can develop a very devastating counter-attack.

. . .

Pivoting is first practiced in a stationary stance, with the bulk of the body weight and thus the balance being transferred from one leg to the other, while shifting body positions. This shifting is often referred to as "Rooting". The idea of rooting keeps the Wing Chun practitioner stable, while being able to change positions easily. After the stationary shifting becomes easier, the student advances to stepping. This will allow the Wing Chun student to effectively use this method while moving forward, backward, to either side, or at a forward or backward angle. With this ability, the ability to fight is greatly enhanced.

Chapter 6

Structure and Energy of The Siu Lim Tao

I n this chapter I will be covering some movements from the first form of Wing chun, the Siu Lim Tao. My intention is not to cover the entire form in this chapter, at least not in the photographs. This is primarily an "ideas" book, not a photo oriented step-by-step manual. There are plenty of those on the market, so really, at this point, who needs another one? There are however, some sections and movements that are in need of clarification, so that's what I will be doing with this chapter.

The Siu Lim Tao

The form begins with a setting up of the Wing Chun training horse stance. Once in this horse stance, there is no further foot movement in the form. The form is performed in a stationary position, while maintaining the training horse stance.

The horse stance is used to develop structural rooted stability and relaxation. It conditions both legs to be the weight supporting leg for our fighting footwork. This stance will also be used to check our moving footwork, much like multiplication is used to check the answer of a division problem in mathematics! This horse stance is preparation for all stances and footwork which will follow in the system.

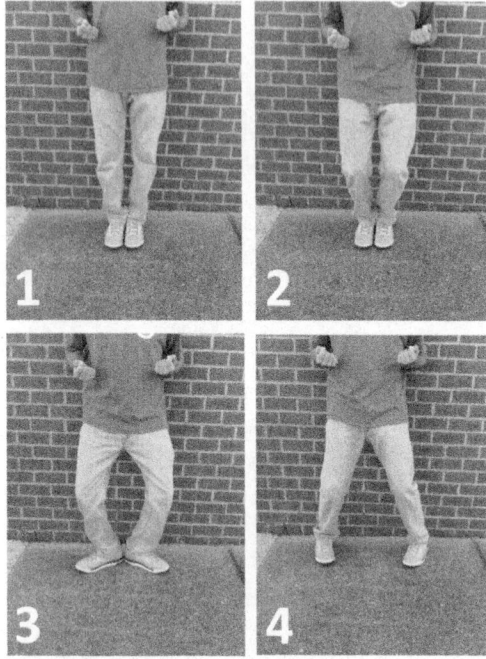

*The opening of the Training stance. 1. Feet together 2.
The Knees bend, keeping the weight on the heels 3.
The toes spread 4. The heels spread wider than thew
toes, with the weight still on the heels, and pelvis
pushed under and forward*

The first section of the form begins to formulate, in the
mind of the student, the structural boundary lines and reference points of one's own body, upon which the movements
of Wing Chun are built. One of the things that Grandmaster Ip Chun said during my training with him was "The
first section is for building the correct energy", that energy is
based on structure and elbow energy.

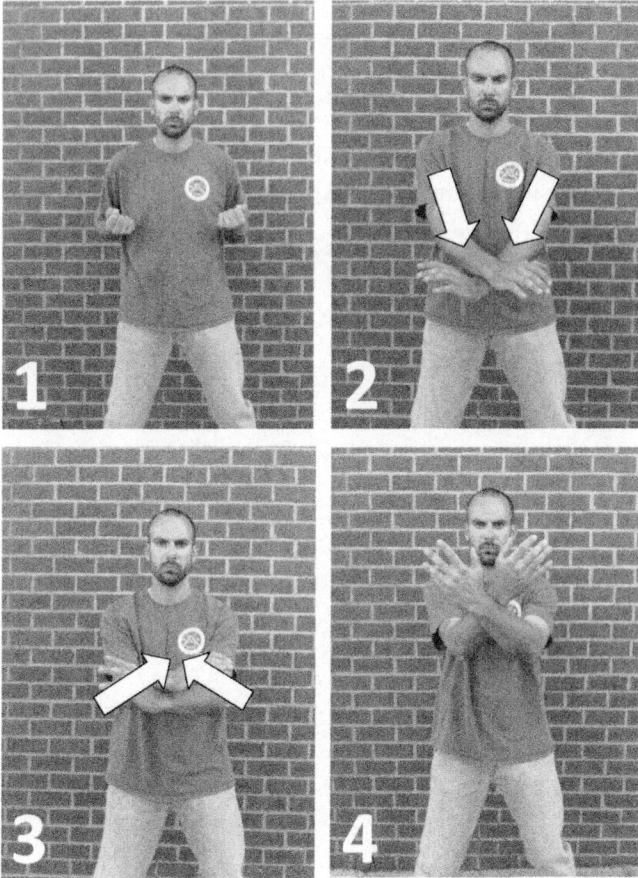

The Crossing low Jaum Sao and Crossing high Gaun Sao define the centerline plane and teach the first two defensive techniques in the Siu Lim Tao. 1. The form begins with both hands in the chambered position. 2. The elbows power the movement as the wrists thrust forward and downward, ending with a crossed wrist position at about navel level, with the palms facing the ground 3. The elbows drop inward causing the entire lower arm to dynamically rotate inward, ending with the wrist crossed in the centre at about shoulder height, with the palms facing the body.

The first defensive hand movements... the downward crossing Jaum Sao, is a movement which thrust from the body, downward and forward, with the focus of the movement being the power of the movement coming from the elbows. (some instructors teach this movement as a downward crossing Gaun Sao, but the downward Gaun Sao is a movement that begins with the hand extended, and cuts back towards the body)

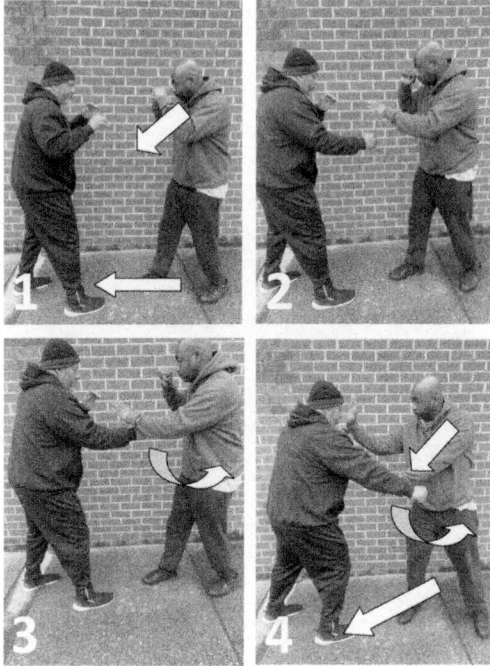

Antonio (R) and Andrew (L) are squared off with one another. Andrew launches a straight right punch to the body. Antonio defends with the low Jaum Sao and simultaneous palm strike to Andrew's face. Note that the Jaum Sao comes forward "from" the guard position, as the centerline shifts from facing Andrew directly, to facing in the direction of Andrew's right shoulder, keeping the structure line of the Jaum Sao on Antonios centerline.

Note the difference in the Gaun Sao from the Jaum Sao shown in the last illustration. As Antonio throws a cross to the hear followed by a low straight punch to the ribs, Andrew defends the high punch with his left hand, then when the low punch is thrown, Andrew's same defensive drops downward and back towards his own body to cover the open low area. The Gaun defends by cutting back towards the body, from an already extended position.

Next is the Upward Crossing Gaun Sao.(and again, some teach this as a crossing Tsun Sao, but this movement is an inward cutting movement, not a pressing movement as in the Taun Sao) These first two movements define the vertical centreline of the body.

The high and low Gaun Sao are sometimes used in combination, called a "Scissors Gaun Sao". The Gaun movement cuts back towards, or with footwork, across, one's own body, from an already extended hand position.

The centreline is a line which bi-sects the body into two equal halves from the top of the head to the floor. But it is not just a vertical line, but a plane which extends from the body out to the full extension of the arm. This imaginary line will be the major reference point for proper structural placement of the blocking and attacking techniques taught in the form.

Centerline Plane

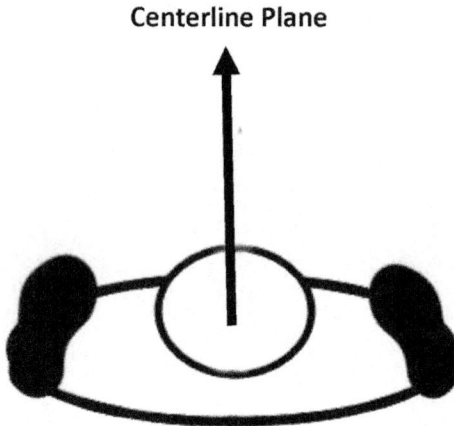

The centreline is not only a line bisecting the body, but a plane which extends to the full extension of the arm, in front of the body.

Each technique in Siu Lim Tao has a proper positional relationship to the practitioners own body. Grandmaster Ip Ching, Ip Man's youngest son, taught a method for building a greater understanding of these structural positions which employs a pole used as a positional reference.

*Grandmaster Ip Ching demonstrating the Siu Lim Tao
with a pole, on the centerline plane, as a reference point
for the placement of the hands for the various thechiques
in the form.*

The pole is placed standing in front of the practitioner, a little beyond the reach of the fully extended punch. The pole is lined up directly in front of the practitioner's center-line. On this pole there are three reference points marked that will correspond with the proper placement in relation to the practitioners body. Point one will be in line with the navel. Point two is in line with where the straight punch lines up at shoulder height. And point three is in line with the eyes. In using this method of training, the practitioner learns the correct position of each of the techniques in the form. He will have a reliable reference of the centerline plane, and learn the proper height of application of each of the techniques.

. . .

In my training with Grandmaster Ip Ching, he emphasised that "each movement of Siu Lim Tao is driven by the elbow. So the elbow is of utmost importance in the training of this form. Movements are either pushed forward or pulled backwards by the elbow, so that is where the student's mind (intent) should be in performing the movements of Siu Lim Tao."

Another thing to keep in mind when learning the form is that every technique is an action (Verb).... not a static position. One big mistake people make in training is that of looking at a "Technique" as an ending static position, and thus miss the angle, and energy that put it in the ending position. Everything that happens from the beginning of a movement all the way through to the ending position is the technique. In each technique, strive to understand the elbow's involvement in pushing or pulling the movement of the technique.

It is this elbow emphasis that most students seem to have a problem with! They can quote that "everything is moved by the elbow" but they seem not to be able to translate the words into movement. This point cannot be over emphasised! Once the student is able to grasp the concept of the elbow being the catalyst for movement they will be well on their way to developing the weapon!

The next movements are the left and right straight punch. This punch is the bread and butter of Wing Chun attacking techniques. There is a maxim in Wing Chun which states that "The punch comes from the heart", in this case, the fist travels on what is known as the "elbow moving line" much like a train travels on its track. The fist is pushed (powered) by the elbow, from its side chamber position to the front, center of the body, where the elbow moving line internets with the centerline plane. This is really the beginning point of the delivery of the punch (in front of the heart). When the fist meets that centerline plane, it begins to travel forward on the centerline, as the elbow continues to push forward, traveling on the elbow moving line.

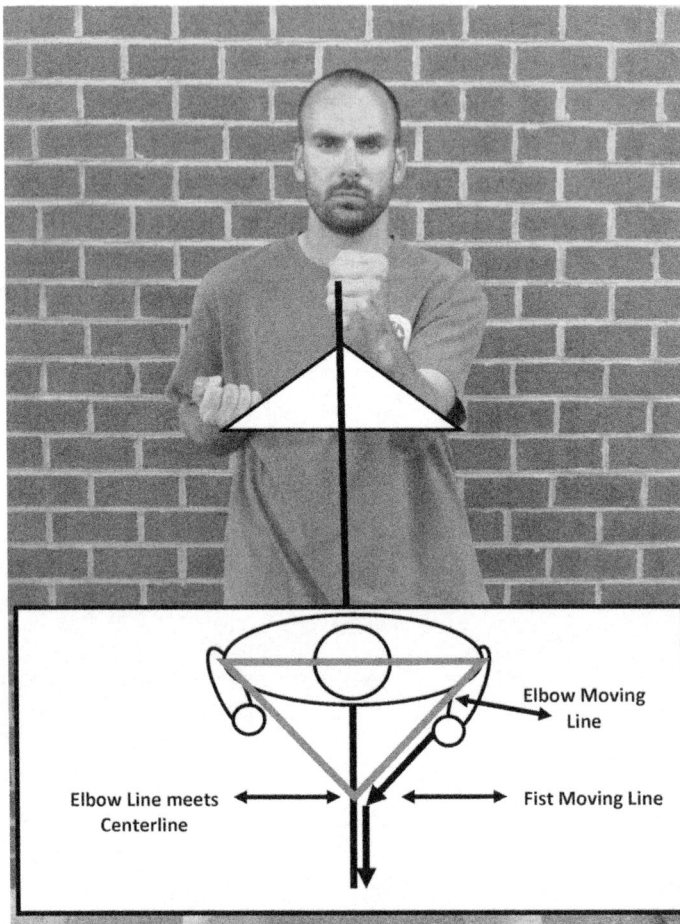

The "Elbow Moving Line" is an extremely important structural "Self Reference Point" in understanding the proper application and power of Wing Chun.

The punch is delivered completely straight. There is no arc to the punch. It travels from (point A) in front of the heart to (point B) the target, in a straight line. The power is in the final few inches of travel. This is the foundation to what has become popularly known as the "Inch Punch" made famous by Bruce Lee.

After delivery of the punch, the hand opens, fully extended, palm up, then performs a circular rotation known as (Huen Sao) Circle Hand, without rotating the elbow, makes a fist and withdraw the hands to chamber.The elbow is not rotated during this movement so that more strain is placed on the ligaments and tendons of the wrist. This is an isometric strength and conditioning movement for the wrist, which tends to be the weak link in delivering the punch.

1. In the form, the punch begins in the chamber position 2. The elbow moves forward following the elbow moving line. The hand is pushed along the same line by the elbow, until it meets, and moves along the centre line plane. 3. The punch reaches full extension 4. The elbow drops put of the punch and the hand opens in a palm up position

5 - 6 The hand begins an inward rotation with the wrist and fingers flexed as far back towards the forearm as possible, while not allowing the elbow to rotate. 7. At the bottom of the rotation, make a fist as well as you can without straightening the wrist. This movement is a great wrist strengthening exercise, as it stretches the ligaments and tendons, thus making the wrist stronger to support the power generated by the Wing Chun punch.

When the left punching sequence is finished, the right hand does the same. The horizontal centerline of the upper body is defined by the left and right punch. This is another body reference point which will become very important in the development of Wing Chun.

The next movements introduced in the first section of the form are a sequence comprised of the Taun Sao, Wu Sao and Fook Sao. Each sequence begins with the left hand and then the sequence will be performed with the right hand after completion of the left hand sequence. These movements are performed in a relaxed manner, with the mind focused on the elbow moving the hand forward on both the Taun Sao and Fook Sao, and pulling the hand back on the Wu Sao. These movements are performed slowly in order to understand and feel the elbow as the catalyst for movement.

This sequence is finished with a side Pak Sao and Straight Palm strike, followed by the same Huen Sao and return to chamber as performed after the punch earlier in the form.

Once the right hand has performed the same sequence of movements, section one of the form is complete.

The next section is a sequence in which both hands are utilized at the same time in performing the movements. In these movements as well as in the opening of the form (the downward crossing Gaun Sao and Upward Crossing Taun Sao) both hands are used for symmetry not application.

· · ·

This section starts with an almost simultaneous left and right side, downward Gum Sao. Next is the rear double low palms followed by the double front Gum Sao. Next is the double Lahn Sao, double side Faak Sao, back to double Lahn Sao followed by a double Jaum Sao double pressing Taun Sao, double Jut Sao, double Biu Gee Sao, double Moot Sao, double Tie Sao, and back to the chambered position.

Once again, the emphasis on the elbow being the focus point of each technique performed is of utmost importance. Without the understanding of the elbow being at the foundation of creating and powering each movement, the form is nothing but an empty dance!

Section three begins with a left hand Pak Sao that crosses the body to the opposite shoulder line. The Pak Sao is followed by a forward, left hand high Side Palm, Huen Sao and return to chamber position. Note that this sequence of movements is taught by different teachers in some differing ways. For example, the Pak Sao is sometimes taught as crossing directly across the body to the opposite shoulder line. Sometime it is taught as following an angled trajectory. Some teachers teach that the forward moving Side Palm moves from its position at the shoulder line with the (left) palm facing three-o'clock on the combat clock directly forward toward twelve-o'clock on the combat clock. Other methods have the Pak Sao hand traveling back to the center of the body before traveling forward to the strike. Still others, have the Pak Sao hand pull all the way back across the body to the side of the body delivering the Pak Sao, using a pulling defensive technique they refer to as an outside Jut Sao. Whichever method is practiced, it is followed by Huen Sao and the withdrawal of the hand to chamber.

Each method has it's reasons and possible advantages and application. I teach each of these variations at some point in my students training. I teach the form as a tool to make the students understanding of Wing Chun and its efficient application better, not as s a silly dance to impress an audience. That being the case, if I have been taught differing variations of the form that have useful strategic and tactical application, I include them in my training program! My end goal is to teach a functional fighting system, not a museum piece passed to my students. I don't want to teach a system that does more to keep a tradition alive than it does to keep my students alive in a violent encounter.

The next part of the has the student perform the pressing Taun Sao after which the hand drops to low Gaun Sao (as shown in the Gaun Sao application example earlier, this is the application from an extended hand position). One of the unique things about the Wing Chun system is that it takes into account defensive and offensive tools from the standpoint that the hand being used may be extended, and thus, need to be applied from that extended position. Gaun Sao is one such defensive tool. If for instance, I have used my right hand to block (Pak Sao) an opponents high left jab, and he quickly withdraws the attacking hand, and redirects his punch to my ribs, I can drop my hand from the extended position and intercept his new attacking line from above with the Gaun Sao. The Taun Sao, Lahn Sao and Bong Sao are other defensive tools that can and in many cases should be applied from an already extended position. Understanding this will take some work on the students part!

In the form the Gaun Sao is followed by a return to Taun Sao (sometimes taught as a Lau Sao or scooping hand) followed by a Huen Sao and Dai Jeung or Low Palm, Huen Sao and withdraw the hand to chamber.

The last section is comprised of the Bong Sao which transitions to the Taun Sao, while keeping the wrist on the centerline, followed by Tok Sao, Huen Sao and chamber. These movements are followed by the left hand shooting forward to downward Jaum Sao, the right hand chambers at the left elbow and performs a (shaving) Jaum Sao, the left and right and left hand follow with the same movements, followed by a left, right, left chain punch, Huen Sao on the last punch and withdraw the hand to chamber.

This completes the Siu Lim Tao form.

Key points to concentrate on in the form are:

Structure - As mention in previous chapters, structure is the foundational component of each technique. You will find some form of a triangular component in many techniques of Wing Chun, from the defensive hands to the stance and footwork. An understanding of the use of the triangular structure as support to the stance or as a wedge in defense is very important.

Jung Saam Sin - the Centerline is the first major concept we learn through the form. We must build body memory for our hands seeking their proper position on the centerline. As Wing Chun practitioners we are to "own" the area directly in front of our body, and learn to protect that area.

Kuen Yau Saam Faat - Punch comes from the Heart, this is the concept of throwing a proper straight punch with the power generated in the final few inches prior to contact. The hand comes from a position in front of the center of the body where the elbow is allowed to continue traveling on the elbow moving line, thus keeping structure behind the punch.

Jie Lik - Borrowing Force, this concept is the key to not fighting force with force. Bruce Lee spoke of 'the art of fighting without fighting" it may be easier to understand this if look at it as the "art of fighting without CONTENDING" We do not contend with the force of the opponent, we borrow it to return it on a more advantageous line of attack for ourselves.

Lat Sao Jik Chung - (Spring forward energy) is the concept of the hand being constantly drawn to the opponent, and if there is nothing to obstruct the path to the opponent, then the hand attacks.

Combat Clock - The combat clock is not a Wing Chun principle or concept, per se, but is an important concept that greatly assist the student with their understanding of direction of movement, or engagement, in an encounter. You hear this concept referenced a lot in the military and in law enforcement. Most readers will be familiar with the statement, "I've got your six" this refers to the person speaking, stating that they are watching your back, which is at the six o'clock position on the combat clock.

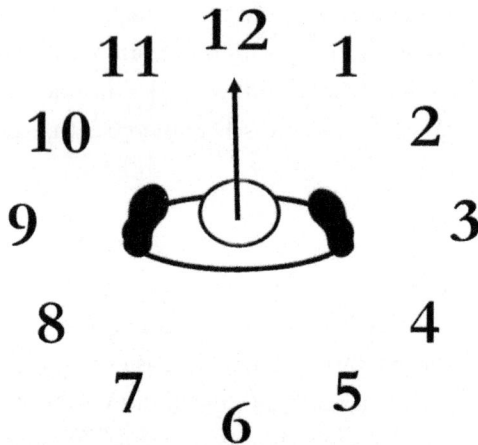

The Combat Clock is a basic principle that when understood can greatly enhance your understanding of footwork and angle of attack and defense.

Chiu Ying - (Facing) The Siu Lim Tao form is performed facing squarely forward toward 12:00 on the combat clock. The body does not shift or turn with any of the movements. This builds body memory for the hands seeking our own centerline plane. This is important because it is used in unison with the concept of Jung Saam Sin - Centerline in a fight.

This training set is designed to "build the weapon" which is you. Once the weapon is functional and reliable, then, and only then, can we think about being able to use that weapon in self-defense against another person. Building the weapon is not enough to make is a useful tool of self-defense. The weapon must be placed on top of a delivery system. That delivery system will be your application footwork, which will come into your training a little along the way in the training drills that teach how to apply the techniques, but in the traditional way of learning Wing Chun, the footwork is added in the second form, Chum Kiu, level of training.

I cover this material in-depth in our Videos, Seminars and Distance Learning program. For information you can visit our web site: www. EfficientWarrior.com

Chapter 7

The Seed Principle

The Combination Principle - The Key to Unchaining your Wing Chun

A technique is a seed from which a lot of applications may grow. The individual technique is a shape, and movement, a direction, an angle, an energy from which we may interpret application in many ways. I always tell my students that "a technique is a structural foundation of an application limited only by your imagination".

Each technique in the system needs to be explored with an eye towards finding as many methods of application as possible. This is the "Unchained" method of looking at the system. Look for striking, defensive and grappling applications of each movement.

. . .

The seed principle is nothing new to Wing Chun. Many instructors will explain that movements like Jeet Kuen (Intercepting punch) is a punching application which has its origin (seed) from the Jaum Sao "sinking elbow defense" or from the cutting angle Pak Sao. The Jeet Kuen as used in Wing Chun does not make an appearance, as such, in any of the Wing Chun forms. But its seed is certainly there.

There are many other techniques which grow out of other seed movements in the system. Some are obvious, while others are less so. Some will take some digging to find, but the treasure is worth the dig!

The Step as a Seed

There is a saying in the Chinese martial arts which states that "a kick is just an exaggerated step". In this saying you can see that any step can be a seed from which a kick may grow. So, with the backward step in the Chum Kiu form, a back kick can be found. From the circle steps in the Biu Gee form, a sweep and hooking kick can be found. The seed of any kick can produce a knee strike. This principle opens the Wing Chun kicking arsenal up to many more methods, directions and angles than are found in the more obvious kicking methods in the system.

The Elbow as a Seed

.   .   .

There are many attacking movements which grow from the "seed" elbow movements of the Wing Chun system.

From the Jaum Sao in the Siu Lim Tao form we get forearm and hammer strikes. From the shifting elbows in the Chum Kiu form we find the seeds of hooking punches as well as turning elbows and hammer strikes. And from the downward hacking elbow in the Biu Gee form we find the seed movement for the very explosive "overhand hook punch" which is used so effectively in Western boxing.

These are just a few of the possibilities found within the Wing Chun system utilizing the seed principle. Now, it is time to do your own homework! One of my mentors in the martial arts, Glen Moore used to tell me, I have shown you A, B, & C .... You will have to explore on your own to find D, E, & F.

The Combination Principle

Just about every Wing Chun technique is based on the combination principle. The Bong/Lop-Da application is a combination of the Bong Sao defense, combined with the Lop Sao and strike, with all of this usually combined with some element of stepping or footwork. This particular application is not found in exactly this combination in any of the forms, but built, much like words from the English alphabet, from individual letters.

Students of Wing Chun are very familiar with the combination principle, however, I feel they are far too limiting in their utilization of this principle. Students of Wing Chun allow their preconceived ideas, or mental pictures of what they think Wing Chun is supposed to look like, limit their use of this principle.

I have had people argue with me when I apply, successfully, a turning back elbow or hammer strike, that there are "NO TURNING TECHNIQUES" in Wing Chun. Now bear in mind these are the same people who are combining a backward angle, or what is sometimes called a back bracing step with a Lop-Da hand combination, which for the life of me I have not found together in any of the Wing Chun forms..... But, I am somehow wrong for combining the back turning step with the turning back elbow application of the shifting Lahn Sao or back turning Fak Sao, all three by the way, found in the second Wing Chun training set, Chum Kiu.

The main argument against this application that I have run into is that Wing Chun is supposed to be Direct and Efficient. They argue that to apply a back turning technique is not direct. To this I will agree ..... if you are attempting to apply this technique when other methods would be more direct. However, there are times when a back-turning elbow, hammer strike of Fak Sao is not only the most direct and efficient; it is also the safest application. For example, if someone were to gain control of your elbow in a fight and is using pressure to gain a positional advantage by flanking you, to attempt to fight his force and regain your fighting position will only leave you vulnerable to his attack for a longer period of time, and waste your energy fighting force against force, from an already compromised position.

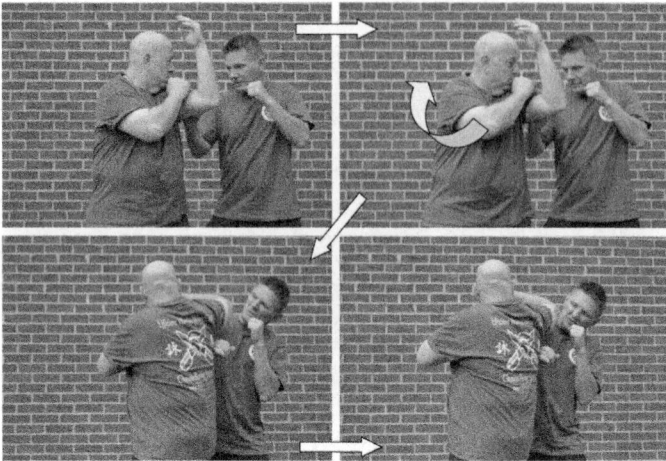

In the above circumstance, the use of the back-turning elbow or hammer strike is the most DIRECT and EFFI-CIENT method which allows you to utilize the opponents force against him, rather than fighting his force, while simul-taneously taking you out of the punching line that the oppo-nent has set up.

For those wanting to expand their understanding and use of the tools of this great system, you need to take this principle and research ALL of the possibilities of use. Unchain Wing Chun from the prison of your preconceptions and the limi-tations you have placed on the system based on what others have said you cannot do. The principle that must remain intact in your exploration is that the application must be Direct and Efficient. But keep in mind that when it comes to the application of a technique in a fight, the judgment of whether it fits this criterion is situational dependent!

Chapter 8

The Wing Chun Straight Punch

The Wing Chun punch, sometimes called the Sun Punch because it resembles the Chinese character for the word Sun, is a very misunderstood technique. Unlike the popular "corkscrew" type punch, delivered with a horizontal fist, found in many systems, the Wing Chun punch is delivered with a vertical fist.

Many systems of Kung Fu, Karate and even Western Boxing utilize the horizontal punch. The Karate Reverse Punch, The Chinese Cantonese Corkscrew Punch and Boxers Jab and Cross all throw with the palm facing the floor, which presents some structural aspects which can be improved upon by simply changing to a vertical fist structure.

Proper Alignment and Structure

To understand the proper alignment and structure of the punch we are going to look at a structure test. This test involves doing a few knuckle push-ups. Anyone coming to Wing Chun after a background in Karate, like the author did, will most likely have done plenty of these push-ups in the past.

Punch Structure Test

We are first going to perform the push-ups in the "Karate" way. First get down in a push up position, on your fist in a Palm- facing -feet position, with the contact point being the knuckles of the index and middle fingers. Now pump off a few push-ups. Do them slowly enough to be aware of the muscles used and power structure of the body during the push-ups.

Next, turn the hands vertical with the palms facing one another. Elbows should be close to the body, with the contact point of the fist and the ground being the middle, ring and pinkie finger. Now do a few push-ups and examine the difference in ease and structure of doing the push-ups in this manner.

That difference is natural alignment and power structure. The vertical push-ups make use of an entirely different muscle group. They allow the body to use the larger and stronger pectorals and abdominal muscles to do the work, where the horizontal push-ups make use of the smaller and weaker triceps and rotary cuff stabilizing muscles. The contact point of the two large knuckles also creates a weaker wrist alignment than that using the lower three fingers of the vertical position.

Not Just Wing Chun

Even the legendary Western Boxer, Jack Dempsey, recognized the superior structure of the vertical punch. In his book, "Championship Fighting - Explosive Punching and Aggressive Defense," published in 1950, Mr. Dempsey explained what he called the "Straight Jolt" a punch he had used with great success.

In the following passage from that great book, Jack

Dempsey explains the "Power Line" and how to test yourself to understand the concept.

The Power Line

The movements in the second part of a straight jolt are just as simple as those in the "falling step"; yet, strangely enough, that part of the punch has been the big blind spot in hitting since the days of Jim Figg in the early 1700's. He was the father of modern boxing.

By the time John L. Sullivan and later "old masters" came along, many outstanding punchers had eliminated that blind spot with their knowledge of punching technique. But today that area of darkness is bigger than at any time since Corbett beat Sullivan.

At least nine of every ten fellows who try to box never become good punchers because they never learn how to make their arms and fists serve efficiently as conveyors and exploders. They become "powder-puff" punchers or, at best, only fair hitters. Their punches lack body-weight, explosion and follow-through.

Such failure can be prevented by power line punching. What is the power line?

THE POWER LINE RUNS FROM EITHER SHOULDER-STRAIGHT DOWN THE LENGTH OF THE ARM TO THE FIST KNUCKLE OF THE LITTLE FINGER, when the fist is doubled. Remember: The power line ends in the fist knuckle of the little finger on either hand. Gaze upon your "pinky" with new respect. You might call that pinky knuckle the exit of your power line- the muzzle of your cannon.

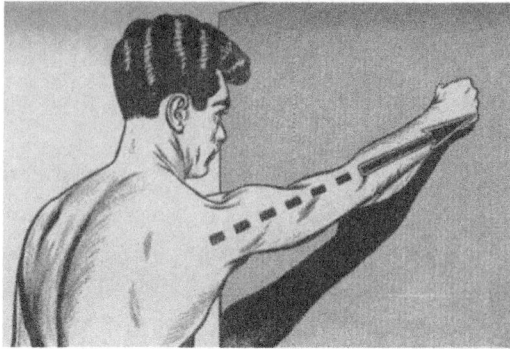

THE POWER LINE RUNS FROM EITHER
SHOULDER-STRAIGHT DOWN THE
LENGTH OF THE ARM TO THE FIST
KNUCKLE OF THE LITTLE FINGER

You'll understand the power line if you feel it out.

Stand up. Walk toward a wall until you're at arm's
length from the wall when facing it. Put your heels together.
You should be standing just far enough from the wall so that
you can barely touch it with the tip of the middle finger of
your right hand-at a point directly opposite your chin.
Touch that chin-high point with your middle-finger tip.

Now, move back three or four inches, but keep the heels
together.

Double your right fist firmly. In making a fist, close the
fingers into the palm of the hand, and then close the thumb
down over the outside of the fingers

Extend the fist at arm's length toward the spot on the
wall-only toward it. The fist should be upright, as if you
were holding a stick running from ceiling to floor. The little
knuckle is down, toward the floor.

With your arm stiffly extended, let your body sway

slowly forward-without moving the feet-until your fist (still upright) is pressed so firmly against the chin-high spot on the wall that your fist and stiff arm are supporting the weight of your leaning body

Note that the lower part of your fist (still upright)-particularly the little knuckle-provides the natural, solid end of the firm, straight line-from shoulder to fist-that is supporting your weight. Note particularly that this line runs unswervingly through your wrist to the little knuckle

Now, with your upright fist still supporting your weight at the chin-high spot, try to shift your pressure from the little knuckle to the upper knuckles. Then turn your fist so that the palm of your hand is down. When you attempt those changes, you should feel immediately that both new pressure position of your fist "lack" the "solidity" of the first position. And you should feel and see that a change in position "swerved" the "power line" at the wrist - putting your wrist in a hazardous landing position.

Keeping your feet in the same position, go through the same procedure with your left fist. You'll find the "power line" in the same location - straight from the shoulder through the little knuckle. But, where would the power line be if you wished to lower your fist and punch at a man's stomach.

You can answer that by testing a spot on the wall just opposite of your own solar plexus - the vital body target just below the end of the breast bone. In making the lower test, sway forward from the same standing position - with either fist - toward the solar-plexus spot. But, before you sway, turn your fist palm down so that the knuckles will be parallel to the ceiling when you press your fist against the wall. The power line still runs solidly through the little knuckle. Now that you have felt out the power line, you can appreciate that the greatest possible solidity would be achieved if you landed every punch with the little knuckle first.

Unfortunately, however, the hand-bone behind the little knuckle is the most fragile of the four bones that support the fist, and s can be broken the most easily. You must not attempt to land first with the little knuckle. Instead you must try to land first with the knuckle next to your pinky (the ring finger). We'll call that the 2nd knuckle. Aiming with the 2nd knuckle usually brings about a three-knuckle landing. Those three-knuckles are: middle, second (ring) and pinky. If you aim with the second knuckle, those three knuckles usually will land together because the average fist slopes slightly from the middle knuckle to the pinky. Such a three-knuckle landing not only prevents the hand-bone behind any one knuckle from bearing all the punch-shock, but it also permits punching almost exactly along the power line. Rarely will one of those knuckles make a solo landing. But if you aim with the little knuckle, you risk a dangerous solo landing on forehead or blocking elbow.

Always aim with the second knuckle-the one next to your pinky-and LET THE OTHER KNUCKLES TAKE CARE OF THEMSELVES. They'll take care of themselves all right; for the shape of the fist makes it impossible for them to do otherwise.

As can be seen above... Jack Dempsey, one of the best punchers in Western Boxing history, advocated a method that it turns out is identical to the Wing Chun vertical punch!

I constantly tell my students that this punch is very misleading to the puncher! It does not "feel" powerful. This is because we are generally conditioned to judge power by how much muscle we "feel" we are putting into the technique! This is not a very reliable indicator of the power in a punch. Structure carries with it its own power! Much like a good Golf swing, it is the structure, alignment and relaxation that brings success. Attempting to muscle through a Golf swing will usually end in a very bad outcome. The same is true with the Wing Chun punch. Besides, the puncher is on the wrong end of the punch to "feel" the power of the punch..... that treat is reserved for the one on the knuckle end of the punch!

Skeletal Anatomy of the Punch

When a punch is delivered, it is powered by the muscles, but the striking surface, the actual weapon, is the bone. Since it is the bones of the hand that suffer the impact of the punch, we need to make sure that we have the best possible skeletal alignment to support the job we expect the punch to accomplish.

In looking at the vertical punch, with the primary contact being with the lower three knuckles, namely the middle, ring and little finger, it is helpful to understand the support structure.

*In the straight punch of Wing Chun, the primary contact surface is
the lower three knuckles, namely the middle, ring and little finger.*

The upper extremity consist of the shoulder (Clavicle
and Scapula), upper arm (Humerus Bone), the forearm
(Radius and Ulna Bones), and the hand (Carpal,
Metacarpals, and Phalangies). The Ulna bone of the
forearm lines up with the lower knuckles of the fist. This
bone ties in with the elbow at the other end.

The fact that the ulna creates the line directly from the
elbow to a point behind the bottom knuckles of the vertical
punch is what gives this punch superior structure.

During a punch which "corkscrews" into a palm down
position the Radius bone actually rotates around the Ulna
with the turn of the wrist, while the Ulna remains in a fixed
position. The Radius bone of the forearm connects on the
thumb side of the hand, in line behind the index and middle
fingers. These two large knuckles are the preferred striking
surface of the horizontal or palm down punch.

99

This method of punching does two things that weaken the structure of the punch. First, it has the striking surface, the large knuckles of the index and middle fingers, supported by the Radius bone, which is not in a fixed structural position, and ties in to the opposite side from the elbow at the joint of the lower and upper arm.

Secondly, the action of delivering the horizontal punch creates an unnatural connection point where the arm connects into the shoulder socket.

The shoulder is a ball and socket joint. When we stand in a natural position, with our hands hanging, relaxed, at our sides, our palms face our body. If we were to raise the arm straight up in front of us, as if to shake someone's hand, the palm will be facing in with the thumb pointing towards ht sky. If you then make a fist, you will be in a vertical punch position. Now if you rotate the fist to a palm down position, it rotates the Radial Bone of the forearm, and rotates the shoulder connection in the ball and socket joint of the shoulder. This creates a structural weakness at the shoulder. Refer back to Jack Dempsey's explanation of the "Power Line" and wall test!

The horizontal punch delivery generally creates the bad habit of "winging the elbow" , which takes the elbow out of structural alignment of the punch, further weakening the punch. With the vertical punch, this is not a problem because it allows the elbow to remain in its "facing the ground" position throughout the delivery of the punch.

Lin Wan Kuen - The Chain Punch

Wing Chun's method of combining straight punches into a "blitz" of punches is called chain punching. Once the first punch has landed on the opponent, the non-punching hand, which will be guarding or covering the opponent's hands, will begin its journey to the target, by following a straight path from its position to the target, without cocking or chambering. The original hand which landed first will simultaneously travel back to the chamber or ready position, on the centerline at a position approximately even with the elbow position of the punching arm, ready to deliver the next punch. This, of course, is combined with aggressive footwork to stay "on top" of the opponent.

The punch is pushed forward by the elbow. After the punch strikes the target, the elbow will fall down and out of the punch as the next punch travels STRAIGHT along the same line simultaneously. As this punch strikes its target, the elbow will fall out of that punch and the next punch will be delivered in the same manner.

A blitz of three to five punches is usually sufficient n this kind of attack. Punching at a rate of about five punches a second ensures a barrage of attacks on the opponent, while at the same time allowing for properly executed punches, with power and structure. Attempting to punch too fast will only weaken the structure and rob the punches of their power.

The punch should always be delivered along a completely straight path to the target. One common mistake is to deliver the punch in a looping or downward circling which drops the punch into its target from above. This is a major mistake. We must always keep in mind that the punch is delivered with the lower three knuckles, supported by the Ulna bone, and delivered from the elbow. This is not possible if the punch is dropping onto its target from above.

This "machine gun" like delivery of the punches ensures that even if the opponent blocks the first punch, another is right behind it.... and another after that!

It has been said that whenever Bruce Lee was serious about a fight he always reverted back to his Wing Chun and utilized the chain punch blitz which he called the Straight Blast.

Training the Punch

Wing Chun used many different training methods to develop the structure, power and speed of the punch. After these attributes are developed the student is further introduced to training methods which will develop reaction and tactical use of this weapon.

Wall Bag Training

The Wing Chun Wall Bag is a basic piece of training equipment that can be invaluable to developing the structure of the punch. Generally there are several ways in which this bag is used. In the first, the bag is hung directly against the wall. The punch is thrown in single, double and triple punch sets. the punch is thrown in a relaxed fashion with the elbow being the focus point of the delivery of the punch. Power should only be used at point of contact. It is important to make sure that the punch travels on a straight line. the returning hand circles under the punching line, and back up into the chamber position, but the punching hand travels the straight line!

In the second method of training on the wall bag, the bag is hung about one to two inched away from the wall. this allows the puncher to punch through the initial contact point and drive the bag into the wall behind the bag. this teaches the often missing element of penetration. When the bag is directly on the wall, there is no real movement of the target upon contact, and thus no feel or understanding of penetration. By being able to punch through the bag into the wall behind it, the puncher learns not to concentrate on the contact point, but to concentrate through the target.

Focus pad training

The use of a focus pad held and manipulated by a training partner is also an important factor in developing the punch as a reliable weapon.

Visual Targeting drill

In a fight, your primary targeting sense is visual. You will have to visually recognize and physically respond immediately when a target presents itself. This eye - hand connection can be trained with the help of a training partner with a focus pad. the drill begins with the partner (the feeder) holding the pad flat against his own chest. when he is ready to present the target, he quickly presents the target for the trainee to strike. The trainee is learning to react to the visually presented target and respond with a good punch as quickly as possible.

Focus Pad Chase

This drill is presented by the feeder in the same way as the previous drill, but this time the trainee will respond with a three or five punch chase.

Elbow Driven Chase vs. Thai Pad

In this drill the feeder utilizes a Thai Pad on the outer forearm. the trainee will be doing a driving chase making contact with the underside of the punching forearm in a cutting action against and driving over top of, and through the Thai pad. The punchers fist are not making contact with anything during this drill. The focus is on the elbow driving the punching arm in a cutting action across the Thai Pad. This drill can dramatically improve the punch like few other training methods!

There are many other training methods for the punch which are designed to develop differing attributes as well as practical application of the punch during training. These presented above will give the student a very good start in the development of Wing Chun's straight punch!

I cover this material in-depth in our Videos, Seminars and Distance Learning program. For information you can visit our web site: www. EfficientWarrior.com

Chapter 9

Don't Punch!

I know ..... I know, I just spent the last chapter describing how to develop the Wing Chun punch! And now I'm telling you not to punch! Well, let me clarify. Be very careful where and when you choose to employ the punch as a weapon. There are times it is good, but there are times and circumstances where it is a very bad idea.

A punch is generally a very sport oriented weapon. By that I mean it is fine when wearing gloves on a fist that has also been wrapped and taped for the protection of the puncher. Without this protection, the fist is very susceptible to injury. And sustaining an injury in a fight for your life is, as you can probably imagine, not in your best interest!

As an example, let's imagine for a moment that you are out with your friends for an evening of fun, but have the misfortune of running into a guy that is out for a different kind of good time, and decides that you are going to be this evenings entertainment. He begins to mouth off at you, but you, having the good sense to attempt to avoid trouble, try to deescalate the situation. As good as your efforts are, he is not in a reasonable frame of mind and the altercation turns physical. You close the gap between yourself and Billy Badguy gaining control of his hands. You see an opportunity and decide to punch this guy in the nose. As you deliver the punch, he flinches forward and down with his head in an attempt to avoid your punch, but you land that sucker despite his efforts. The problem is, instead of connecting with his pointy little nose, your fist crashes into his forehead, the hardest bone structure in the human body. His forehead just became the windshield, and your hand, the bug!

As a police officer, as well as in my time as an emergency medic, I responded to a countless number of fights. I have seen many broken hands and boxer's fractures, with the owners of those broken tools having other injuries sustained after their hand was broken and pretty much became useless, or at least a very painful hindrance to its use an a tool for offense or defense.

If a punch is used as a striking tool to the head, it is much better to target the side of the head in the region of the ear, or behind the jaw line. I always advise my students to avoid its use to the frontal area of the face. As mentioned earlier there is the danger of connecting with the forehead or worse in my opinion, the teeth.

Connecting with the opponents teeth with the bare fist almost always results in the fist being cut by the teeth. The mouth is a very dirty thing, and I'm not just referring to "Master" Wong's language .... The human mouth is full of germs, not to mention blood-borne pathogens like HIV/AIDS and Hepatitis. So a punch to the mouth may win the battle, at the expense of losing the war, so to speak.

Punches are much more suitable for striking the body. Targets such as the ribs, kidney and solar plexus are much more suitable for the use of the punching tools. From a Wing Chun perspective, the empty hand tools are taught and developed through the training in the three forms, Siu Lim Tao, Chum Kiu and Biu Gee. After or sometimes during the time these forms are taught, the student learns the Mook Yun Jong, or wooden dummy form. The dummy takes the place of having a training partner, and teaches methods of applying the tools learned in the other forms, against an opponent. In examining the dummy form you will find that punches are not directed towards the area of the dummy which would represent the face. Only open hand weapons such as the palm strike, the side chopping hand or thumb gouge is used to that area. You will, however find the punch applied to the section of the dummy that represents the body. In police work ..... they call that a clue!

An open hand is a much more versatile tool for attack than the fist. I was once told by an instructor, and please forgive me, I do not remember which one, as you look back over fifty years of instruction, sometimes the message is remembered, but the messenger becomes a foggy memory, but to my point, I was told "the fist is only good for two things, knocking on doors and knocking on people, and not all that good at the knocking on people part". An open hand can palm, gouge, grab and control. A fist is nothing more than a club.

*The open hand is a much more functional weapon
than the fist in attacking the face of the opponent.
Nothing say's "leave me alone" quite like a Thumb in
the Eye!*

Hooks and Uppercuts - The neglected tools of Wing Chun

The Wing Chun system system is a very versatile martial system, but is very often diminished in effectiveness by the neglect of many of its tools. A great example of this is the neglect of training and utilizing the hook and uppercut punches of the system.

When we look at western boxing, we see the straight punches, the jab and cross, used in combination with the hook and uppercut. The straight punches set up the hooks and uppercuts, and the hooks and uppercuts set up the straight punches! It's a marriage made in heaven!

So you may ask, why is it that we don't see Wing Chun fighters utilizing these tools? I have been asking that question for years. I have come to the conclusion that most people don't use them because they don't fit into their mental view of what Wing Chun is supposed to "look" like.

Too many people get their idea of how Wing Chun is applied by watching kung fu movies, or worse .... YouTube! If you looked at what many instructors present as application of the system, you would think Wing Chun is the art of standing like Donnie Yen, while wearing a silly Chinese Gown, and chain punching people to death!

To limit Wing Chun to just the straight punches is like having a six-shot revolver and choosing to only load two of the chambers! Don't make that mistake! Open that Wing Chun tool box and learn to utilize as many of the tools as possible!

Chapter 10

Facing, Triangular Structure and Fook Sao

F acing, Triangular Structure and Fook
Sao.... Keys to understanding Wing Chun
Application

Wing Chun is a combat system based on concepts and
principles which make it direct, efficient and effective.
Among the principles which form the foundation upon
which Wing Chun is based are those of Facing and the
Triangular Structure, which are interrelated and integral to
the understanding of how Wing Chun works.

As explained in a previous chapter, the opening movements of Wing Chun's first form, the downward and lifting
crossed hands define the vertical centerline and introduce
the systems foundational triangular structure. A thorough
study of these two principles will greatly enhance the Wing
Chun students understanding of practical application and
the economical structure for which this system has become
famous!

The principle of "Facing" uses the Centerline (covered
in chapter six) the first self-reference point in the system. In
understanding the centerline as a plane which extends out

from the body, and moves with the body. The Centerline plane forms the apex of both forward and reverse triangular structures used as references by the Wing Chun fighter. The student will develop, through training, a conditioned reflex to keep their centerline covered. They will learn to apply the centerline Facing - as well as Forward and Reverse Triangle principle against both circular attacks and straight line attacks for the best structural advantage.

THE COMBAT CLOCK

I make use of what is known as the combat clock in teaching physical movement. This teaching method makes it much easier to visualize, in the mind's eye, direction and angles as well as footwork and facing. The combat clock is a teaching tool that has been lost in recent generations due to the development of the digital clock. I remember attempting to use this principle with a youth group, and they looked at me like a socialist at a job application! They had no idea What it was!

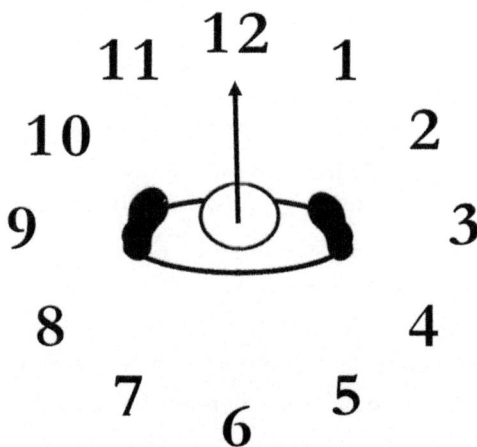

Picture yourself as standing in the center of a clock. Twelve o'clock is directly in front of you. Three is to your right, nine to your left and six directly behind you. Using this method will help you visualize the way situations are presented in the remainder of this book!

In a circular attack, if we consider the attacker to be at the 12:00 position on the Combat Clock, by making use of the reverse triangle, the Wing Chun fighter will shift to face 11:00 against the attack coming from their left side, or to 1:00 for an attack coming from the right. The defending hand will move forward along the centerline to protect the body with the most naturally strong structure, while simultaneously striking with the other hand.

In a straight line attack, the Wing Chun fighter will move the centerline in an intercepting angle with the incoming punch, using the forward triangle, into the core of the attackers body. The defense can be performed with either hand, with the other hand used for the counter-offensive strike.

In teaching this method we use a drill we call the "Compass Man"

in which the student develops an understanding of the use of the extremely economical triangular structure. In the same way that the hand of the Compass always points to the North... the Wing Chun fighters hands, in this drill, will always form the triangle, converging one's own centerline.

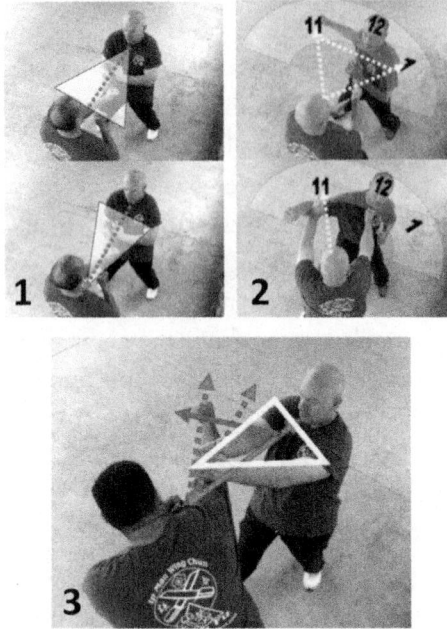

In these images we see 1. the Forward and Reverse Triangle structures 2. The use of the Reverse Triangle structure in combination of the use of the Combat Clock to understand proper angles and 3. The Forward Triangle as used in the Compass Man Drill

In this drill, the Wing Chun fighter will learn to utilize this triangle to intercept and overcome the opponents punch with proper "facing" structure. in this method, the fighter learns to use their triangular structure as a wedge to overcome the attack and gain a position of advantage, without the over-use of muscular strength.

The next movements within the first section of the Siu Nim Tao (Young Idea) form, is a sequence of Fook and Wu Saus.

This sequence actually begins with a Taun Sau,- Wu Sao followed by three sets of Fook and Wu Sau hands, completed by a side Pak Sao and Straight Palm.

In teaching methodology we learn that the number of times something is repeated in the learning process often gives insight as to the importance of that element. This being true, we should take a close look at the Fook Sao and Wu Sao in this first section of the form, as they are the most repeated defensive movements... not only of the first section, but in the entire form.

The first of these two movements to make an appearance in the form is the Wu Sao. We encounter the first Wu Sao following the Taun Sao. After this it is repeated after each of the three Fook Saos. The fact that this particular technique is the most repeated movement in the entire first form, I believe speaks volumes as to how important the Wu Sao is to the Wing Chun method.

The Wu Sao serves two purposes. One is passive, as a guarding hand when the other hand is engaged. This is very important because in many other systems, we see the "non-active" hand withdrawn to the side of the body where it is useless for all practical purposes. The use of the Wu Sao as a guarding hand builds the understanding of the importance of remaining in a good protective posture at all times. As well as having the hand in the best possible position to launch an attack.

The second use of the Wu Sao is as an active blocking hand. The structural shape of the Wu Sao makes it very formidable in intercepting an attack thrown in a circular manner with heavy force. It is actually much less likely to collapse under heavy force than the Taun Sao that is usually seen as the defensive tool of choice of many against a hooking punch. A little experimentation of both the Wu

Sao and the Taun Sao used under these conditions will prove this to be true!

The next most trained defensive technique in the form is the Fook Sao. The Fook Sao has several fighting principles attached to its use. Wing Chun is a very conceptual fighting system. Often the use of the tools Taught in the forms is limited only by the students understanding and imagination. I often tell my students that "A technique is the physical foundation of an application, limited only by your imagination". I am always telling them to "Ask not what the technique is.... rather ask, WHAT ALL could it be". Much like a screwdriver can be used as a chisel, a pry bar, a bridge extension between a nail and a hammer, for driving the nail.... as well as for driving screws, each technique can have many uses!

One of the major principles tied to the Fook Sao is that of Chiu Ying (facing). In order to apply the Fook Sao properly as a defensive tool, one must be properly facing the opponents attack!

In training, I usually teach my students to use the Fook Sao as the first technique in intercepting the straight line punch. This teaches the student to properly face the attacker. The use of a Pak Sao or Taun Sao give the student the opportunity to defend the attack without using proper facing, as the Pak Sao can cross the centerline allowing a block without facing the attacker... the Taun Sao can also be applied much like a Karate outside block, (facing Photo) moving laterally across the punching line, without properly facing the attacker. Neither of these applications are proper but can be used successfully, many times without the student realizing that they are using improper structure.

The Fook Sao, on the other hand, cannot be used unless the student is properly facing the attacker. For this reason, I feel it is a very good starting point in teaching the Wing Chun student to intercept the straight punching line.

Once the Fook Sao in well understood, the student can then utilize the same facing posture, with the use of triangulation, like the bow of an Ice-Breaking Ship, and learn to use the Pak Sao and Taun Sao accompanied with a counter-offensive strike to overcome the straight line punch. In teaching the Fook Sao first, the student learns the proper structure for many of the other techniques, which could easily be done wrong without first developing the structure required in Fook Sao.

Applications of techniques with improper structure can work in a training environment, with a compliant training partner, but will only cause the student to develop a false sense of security! Proper training on structure and well understood principles of application are what is needed when facing violent aggression.

Remember..it's not practice that makes perfect.... it's proper practice that makes perfect!

Chapter 11

Wing Chun Kicking

W ing Chun Kicking - Beware What Lies Below the Surface.

Wing Chun is a Southern Chinese Kung Fu system best known for its extremely effective close range fighting methods. Being that it specializes in the close range environment, Wing Chun's hand techniques are what most people notice about the system. Wing Chun is so well known for its hand techniques that many martial artist from other systems seek instruction in Wing Chun in order to enhance their fighting ability. They find it a good way to enhance their training in other systems which emphasis kicking techniques. But much like an iceberg, there is much more below the surface of this system than is visible at first glance. Those who are able to look below the surface of Wing Chun will find the hidden treasure of the system, a highly effective method of using the legs as both a defensive and offensive tool.

Many martial systems have very impressive kicking methods which include kicks to the head, jumping, spinning and high flying verities.

Wing Chun on the other hand primarily utilizes kicking methods in unison with the close range hand techniques, thus requiring most of the kicking methods be simple, and effective at close range. Rarely will one see a Wing Chun fighter applying a kick to a high target area.

Generally Wing Chun teaches that the legs take care of the lower body, and the hands take care of the upper body (offensively). And legs take care of legs; hands take care of hands (Defensively).

This principle can be applied in several ways, and has many advantages for the Wing Chun fighter. First of all, when you use legs to the lower body, your balance is easier to maintain compared to methods of kicking to the upper body or head. Flexibility is not as much of a factor, and the target areas you are attacking are much more difficult for the opponent to defend, there is also the added benefit that the lower body targets are much weaker that targets of the upper body.

Kicks to targets like the ankle or knee cab be delivered from close range, and simultaneously with the use of the hands to control or attack.

This is not to say that high kicks can't be made to work. Anyone who has trained long enough to develop the timing, speed, skill, and flexibility of a good Black Belt can possibly use these techniques effectively. But the effectiveness of a martial art system is better judged by how fast the beginning student can learn to protect themselves with the method being taught. My first Wing Chun teacher, Duncan Leung, used to say "it makes as much sense to reach down and punch the opponent in the toes as it does to raise the leg up to kick him in the nose".

*High kicks expose your lower targets to counter attack.
Lifting the leg that high to kick leaves all you hold
dear "hanging" in the balance!*

For this reason and the fact that Wing Chun was origi-
nally developed as a combat system, and has no sporting
application, Wing Chun prefers to keep the kicks low.

Defensively, Wing Chun teaches to primarily use legs
to defend against low kicks applied by the opponent, and
low kicks as counter offensive weapons against opponents
attacking with high kicks. Hand defensive techniques are
usually applied against the hand attacks of the opponent. If
you have been around the martial arts for any length of
time, you have likely seen demonstrations and magazine
articles where the defender is able to defend against a
punch by kicking the arm that is punching. While this may
make for an impressive demonstration, the chances of it
working in a non-choreographed situation, where the
attacker is not cooperating with the defender, is a bigger
long shot than CNN doing a positive story about Donald
Trump!

First of all, if there is distance and time to recognize the attack, and get the leg up high enough to block a punch that the attacker has thrown, the attacker has thrown a punch from so far away that there was probably no need to block it in the first place. Add to this the fact that a punch launched from that far away is much easier and more effectively defended by a counter offensive kick which will catch the attacker during the delivery of the punch.

Wing Chun teaches that if we use the hands to defend against hand attacks; we will be well balanced, and better able to launch a counter offensive technique. The same is true with kicking techniques. The leg is much stronger than the arm. Blocking a strong kick with the arm is at best a gamble. The legs are much more capable of handling the force of a kick attack than are the arms. One other advantage of using the legs to defend against kicks is that it leaves our hands free to launch an immediate counter offensive attack. This also leaves you at a range that the kicker will find it difficult to effectively launch a second kick. The legs can be used to jam the kicking line of the opponent, or can be used to pick off the kick much like our Patriot Missiles were used against the Scud missiles in the Gulf War.

Another advantage of the leg defending the kick is that the leg defense generally affects the opponents balance more that attempting to block with the hands. This leaves the opponent more vulnerable to attack, and less capable of launching an effective second attack.

Naturally, it will not always be possible to apply this method. There will be times when the Wing Chun fighter will have to defend a kick with the hands. There will be times when we may be caught off balance or in an awkward position. In dealing with multiple opponents, it will be impossible to be in the perfect position to defend any attack when you don't know which opponent will be launching the attack. For those instances when the Wing Chun fighter may have to use the much weaker hand technique to defend against a strong kick, we have the second principle that we will utilize.

That principle states that you should " stop the attack as close to the point of origin as possible". In Wing Chun we use this principle in defending with either the legs or the hands, but it is this principle specifically that allows the Wing Chun fighter to use the hands against the much stronger leg attacks of an opponent. There are several advantages in understanding this principle.

This principle keeps the Wing Chun fighter from having to deal with the maximum power of a technique. To help us understand this principle, let's compare a Round-house Kick to the human lifecycle, the birth and maturation of man.

Try to imagine that you are facing an opponent. But not just any opponent. Picture in your mind's eye the biggest, toughest, meanest, most skillful opponent you can think of. If this opponent launched an attack, let's say a Roundhouse Kick, it will probably be a very powerful kick, which will be difficult to stop, and will do a great deal of damage if it lands. Now, picture yourself facing that same opponent, only this time he is only about five years old. If he launches that same attack, how difficult do you think it would be to stop? At this age he will not have had the time to develop the skill to kick effectively, and at the age of five he will not be that big, tough or strong. In this scenario you will have caught him before he grows and matures. It works the same way with defending against attacks.

The physical birth of a Roundhouse Kick begins at the moment the opponent begins to shift his weight in order to get in the proper position to launch the attack. As the knee begins to rise, and point at the intended target, this can be compared to the kicks childhood. When the lower leg begins to rotate around the Knee joint, approaching impact with the intended target, the kick is reaching maturity. The Kick striking the target has become fully-mature. Much like the example given above, the earlier in the lifecycle you are able to face the attack, the less capable it will be able to do you harm. If you disrupt the opponent as he is shifting his weight in order to kick, he will be unable to launch the kick. If you are able to make contact with the hip or upper leg just as he is chambering the leg to launch the kick, he will be unable to kick. If you make contact with the knee just as the lower leg is beginning its rotation around the Knee joint, you will be able to take the majority of the power out of his kick.

If you make contact with the knee just as the lower leg is beginning its rotation around the Knee joint, you will be able to take the majority of the power out of his kick.

But as the Kick begins to mature, if you make contact with the kick between the knee and the foot, you will have to deal with the power of the kick at full maturity. The closer the kick gets to its intended focus point, the more power the kick will have.

There is one other advantage to taking the kick on early in its development. If you focus on blocking the kick at or near the foot, you will not only be absorbing the power of the kick, it will be much harder to determine just where to block the kick. A good kicker can kick you anywhere from the ankle to the top of your head. This can leave you having to cover an area of over six feet. That's a lot of real estate to protect. Especially when you have no idea as to which target he will attack. Compound this with the ability of some kicking specialist to change targets in mid-kick, and you can imagine the defensive challenges you may be facing. This problem is virtually eliminated when you apply the principle of stopping the attack at or near the point of origin.

Any kick the opponent will throw, no matter what his intended target, will originate at his hip. If you focus your defensive efforts, by way of your own disruptive kick to the opponents hip area, you can shut his kick down at its birth.

Using the legs to defend against kicks is that it leaves our hands free to launch an immediate counter offensive attack. This also leaves you at a range that the kicker will find it difficult to effectively launch a second kick.

This Principle is not limited to dealing with kicks; it will also work against hand attacks. As long as you examine a technique, and understand the lifecycle of the attack, no matter what form that attack may take, you will be able to utilize this principle. While these are not the only principles dealing with Wing Chun's leg techniques, they will make it much easier to understand why Wing Chun kicking is so effective.

While Wing Chun is well known for the more visible aspects of the system, like Chi Sao, chain punching, the wooden dummy, and double knife techniques.... it's not always what is seen that you

have to worry about! it's the lesser known kicking methods that could very well be the most damaging weapons of the system, after all, it wasn't the visible tip of the iceberg that sank the Titanic!

Chapter 12

Spies in the enemy's camp

Wing Chun's Chi Sau and Building Bridge Contact!

" Hence it is only the enlightened ruler and wise general who will use the highest intelligence of the army for the purpose of spying and thereby they achieve great results".
Sun Tsu

Spying is by far the greatest asset of intelligence an army can have. Spies can keep their side abreast of troop movements, strategic plans, and which weapon the enemy plans to use. Indeed, if you are able to implant spies, you are well on your way to victory.

The Chinese Kung Fu system of Wing Chun operates on this principle like no other. Chi Sau (Sticking Hands) is a training method unique to Wing Chun. This method trains the Wing Chun practitioner to create contact between himself and his opponent. This contact is called building a bridge. Once this bridge contact is created, the Wing Chun practitioner will receive information by way of the sensory nerves. He will be able to read pressure, angle, movement, even subtle shifting of weight in the opponents stance which can give him forewarning as to the intensions of the opponent. This can be compared with having spies in the enemy's camp.

Chi Sau encompasses the possible contact relationships between two fighters. When both hands are in contact with each other, there are three possible relationships.

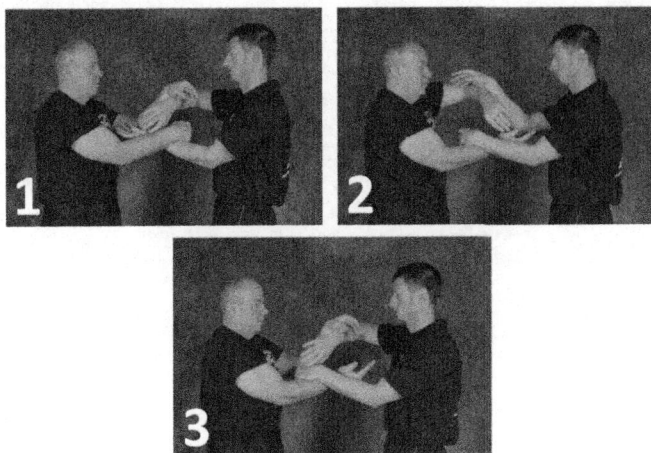

1. Both hands on the outside of the opponents 2. Both hands on the inside of the opponents 3. One hand inside and one hand outside of the opponents.

Both hands on the outside of the opponents
Both hands on the inside of the opponents

One hand inside and one hand outside of the opponents.

In single hand contact there are four possible relationships.

1. Same side inside position 2. Same side outside position 3. Cross side inside position 4. Cross side outside position

Same side inside position
  Same side outside position
  Cross side inside position
  Cross side outside position

All of these possible relationships are covered within the scope of Chi Sau training. Practitioners learn how to interpret sensory input they receive from the opponent and develop proper reactions to what they feel.

Bridge Contact – the key to Chi Sau application in combat

There is a maxim in Wing Chun that says that "the fighter is to seek the bridge, and if there is no bridge, build one"! The building of this bridge becomes very important once skill in Chi Sau has been attained. According to Grandmaster Ip Ching, the son of Bruce Lee's teacher, Ip Man, Chi Sau is the genius of Wing Chun. Chi Sau is the key to the use of Wing Chun in a real fighting situation. And that is the chief focus of Wing Chun training, application of technique in fighting.

The basic structure of Chi Sau

There is a cyclic structure between two Chi Sau practitioners. One cycle is that of the inside position which rolls form Taun Sau to Bong Sau with both hands. Another cycle is that of the outside position which rolls from low Fook Sau to high Fook Sau. The third cycle is that of one hand inside and one hand outside in which both cycles are performed by both trainees, based on the individual hand relationship. Within these rolling cycles the trainees must maintain protection of their center by way of proper hand position and proper direction and amount of pressure exerted. This is a tricky process, as it is very easy to lose position during the rolling exchange of hand position. It is this training that prepares the Wing Chun fighter for the dynamic contact phase of a violent encounter.

.   .   .

Within each of these hand position relationships, certain attacking and trapping possibilities present themselves. The trainees will use these attacks to train each other how to react in a precise and economical manner. Wing Chun is based on economy of motion, so the responses must be trained and refined until they have no extra or wasted motion. This also makes the response automatic body memory.

Body memory is important, as it has been discovered that we do indeed react the way we train ourselves to react. In teaching Law Enforcement we have found that this is very important.

Two examples from Law Enforcement have taught us just how important body memory is. There is one case from Canada where a uniformed constable who was a defensive tactics instructor, was shot in the shoulder by a criminal in the street. The tragedy of this is, that the criminal shot the officer with a gun that had been successfully taken away from him with a flawless gun disarm by the constable, and then automatically returned to the criminal by the constable due to the fact that the constables training had made both the disarm and the return of the firearm "body memory". In training, the officers would perform the disarm, and imme-diately return the gun to their training partner so that they could perform the disarm again and again. Under stress, body memory takes over, and performs as the body has been taught to react.

The second example we have from Law Enforcement is truly sad. In a shoot out with some bank robbers, several police officers were killed. In the post-incident investigation, one of the diseased officers was found to have several empty shell casings in his hand. On the shooting range the police officers had been taught to pick-up their shell casings. Under stress, this officer had done as he had trained his body to do. He was bending down and picking up his empty shell casings while in a gun fight with his life on the line. If this can happen to a professional law enforcement officer, it can also affect the martial artist.

In the book "Psycho - Cybernetics" there is an explanation of what the author, Dr. Maxwell Maltz, calls the four stages of learning. These four levels explain the way the mind works in learning a skill. Dr. Maltz explains that there is a progression from knowing nothing of the skill, to mastery of the skill. These four levels of learning represent a natural process that can be seen to be present in any physical skill development.

In the area of developing skills of personal protection, an understanding of these four levels gives the practitioner a very good idea of when they can expect a fighting skill to be something they can really rely on when if they are the victim of a violent attack.

Dr. Maltz explains the four stages of learning as follows:

The four levels of learning are:
    Unconscious Incompetence
    Conscious Incompetence
    Conscious Competence
    Unconscious Competence

. . .

As we study these four levels, you will see the natural progression of skill development. When we are a beginning student of the Martial Arts, we may enter training with the misconception that we understand how to perform a rudimentary skill such as punching. However, we quickly learn just how wrong we are when we begin to learn the details required in delivering a proper punch. We learn that there are many important elements that must be learned and coordinated in order to deliver an effective punch, such as proper structural alignment of the shoulder, elbow and fist. Developing a proper base through which power is generated and delivered into the punch. Learning how not to telegraph our intention to throw the punch in order to have the opportunity of actually hitting the opponent, and several other important factors. We quickly realize that we never really knew how to deliver a proper punch.

It is with this realisation that we pass from level one: Unconscious Incompetence, to the second level: Conscious Incompetence. We have now discovered that we do not know what we thought we knew about delivering a punch. This is when we begin the process of learning the proper mechanics of punching. Once we develop an understanding of the proper mechanics of throwing the punch, and find that we are able to reproduce satisfactory results in delivering the punch, we have passed from level two into level three: Conscious Competence. But wait.... it's not time to celebrate yet. The technique will not be reliable, under real world stressful conditions until you graduate to level four!

In a real fight there is no time to think. What is needed is reaction. So your ability to perform the technique and reproduce satisfactory results in training does not mean you can rely on it in self-protection just yet. In order for the technique to be reliable, you must have entered the fourth level of learning, Unconscious Competence. This is when you will experience "Conditioned Reflex" in your technique. This is when the technique "performs itself", without your mental deliberation or intent.

You cannot rush the learning process. Impatience can be a serious character defect in Kung Fu. Grandmaster Ip Chun warns "Everything in nature has its timing. When you plant a seed, you water it, give it sunlight, nurture it. As time passes you begin to see the plant grow. If you pull on the plant to help it grow, you will damage it rather than help it. The same is true of your Kung Fu training. The term Kung Fu means "Energy and Time" it takes both to master Wing Chun."

It is not until the practitioner reaches the fourth level with their techniques that he can rely on them in a dynamic encounter. The Chi Sao exercise is unequaled in building students martial skills to the fourth level.

Chi Sao is the ultimate in training the body to react, on its own, appropriately, in a dynamic encounter. As skill in Chi Sao is developed, the trainee will feel more like a spectator rather than an actor in the action. It is not unusual to hear two Chi Sao trainees discuss what just happened during an exchange with the statement "I'm not sure what I did, it happened so fast that I didn't do the movement, "IT" did the movement"

Immobilising the Hands

In each of the Chi Sao relationships, there are a number of ways to immobilize the opponent's hands. Immobilising the hands leaves the opponent defenseless against attack. Grandmaster Ip Ching points out that it is control of the opponent that is the skill of Chi Sao, "Just because you can hit the opponent, doesn't mean you can control him, but if you can control him, you can hit him at will!" It is this control that makes immobilising or trapping, which is a term Bruce Lee made popular for this Wing Chun concept, such an important skill.

I remember a conversation between myself and my student Jason Korol (world famous, best selling Wing Chun and Jeet Kune Do author .... By way of full-disclosure, he paid me to say that) about someone making a statement that "trapping can't be used in a fight, name anyone who has ever successfully used trapping in a fight". I remember telling Jason, "you see it all the time, it's the most reliable defense in western boxing, they call it a "clinch".

The following will explain several immobilisation methods utilized in fighting , which come from each of the positions within Chi Sao.

Immobilisation from the inside position

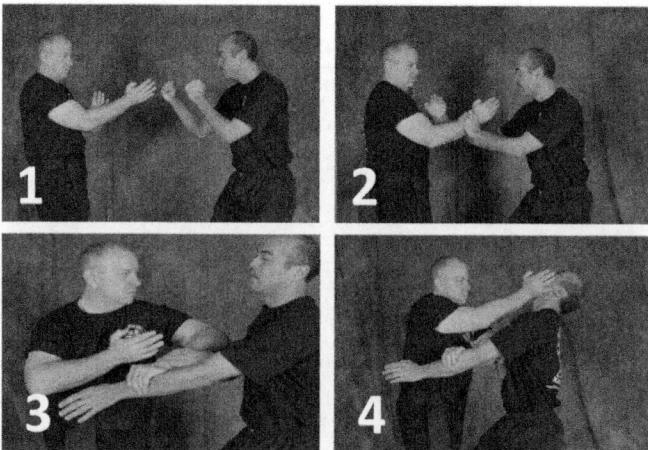

In this sequence Lafayette Harris creates the bridge contact by seizing both of Massengill's hands in an attempt to control him. Massengill applies a left Gear Trap to Lafayette's right arm while simultaneously controlling his left arm with the same arm, leaving his right free to launch an attack to the head.

Immobilisation from the outside position

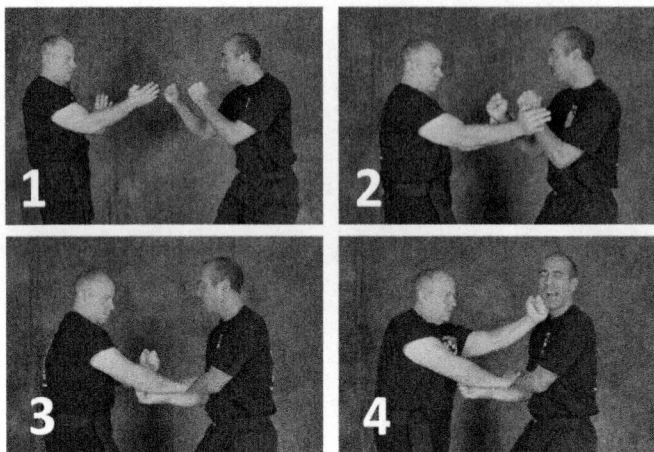

In this sequence Massengill closes to a double outside bridge. He then uses Lafayette's left hand to trap his right hand, clearing the path for a straight punch to the jaw.

Immobilisation from one hand inside and one hand outside

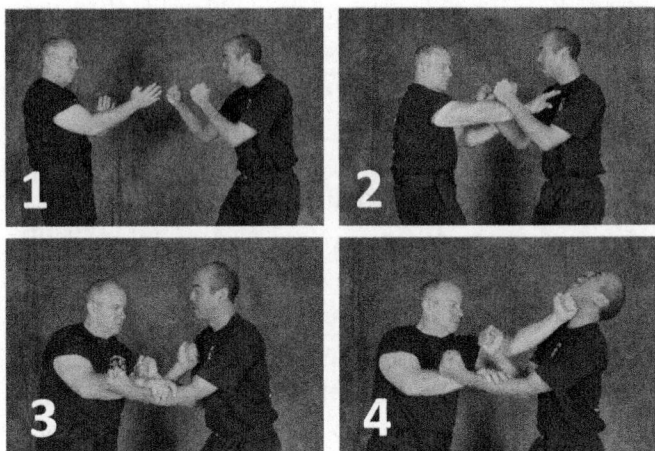

In this sequence Massengill closes to bridge with a left hand Gum Sao (Pressing hand) and right hand Biu Taun Sao (Thrust-Spreading Hand). Massengill then applies a simultaneous control of Lafayette's left arm while applying a cutting punch which controls the right hand during his attack. He then follows up by using his left arm to control both of the opponent's hands while applying a right straight punch.

As can be seen from the above illustrations, Chi Sao is a very effective training method in building the skill of controlling the opponent. And as in any good training method, there is an ever increasing skill level built in to the drill.

Bruce Lee himself in a book he wrote on Wing Chun, and gave the writing credit to his friend J. Yimm Lee, compared Chi Sao to the Paper, Rock, Scissor game we played as children, there is always a way out of what the opponent does, as long as you react correctly. Chi Sao teaches the reactions to be automatic, directed by the sensory input from the contact in the bridge positions.

Chi Sao is often taught in response cycles. In a single response cycle, trainee one will initiate a technique, Trainee Two will respond, and this is the end of the exchange. A double response cycle will have Trainee One deal with Two's response with a counter. Techniques are often taken through a triple response cycle. Beyond this is Gor Sao (Free-Flow) Chi Sao. At this level Chi Sao becomes a game of physical Chess. One in which anyone can initiate any attack. There are no pre-set techniques or responses, and the action is very fast and dynamic.

It is interesting that in Bruce Lee's last finished movie, Enter the Dragon, he was still explaining the "Highest Form of Technique" in the same terms he used in his notes many years earlier, to explain Wing Chun's Chi Sao method. In the sequence in which Bruce is questioned by his teacher in the garden after the opening fight sequence with Sammo Hung, Lee's teacher ask him "What is the highest form of technique?" Lee responds "To have no technique" in explanation he states" When the opponent expands, I contract, when he contracts, I expand. And when there is an opportunity to attack, I don't hit, "IT" hits all by itself" This is the same explanation which can be found in the book "The Tao of Gung Fu" by Bruce Lee. The quotation can be found in the chapter on Chi Sao!

The Misuse of Chi Sao

As good as Chi Sao is in its development of conditioned reflex, it has its limitations! This is where many Wing Chun practitioners go wrong! The legendary Samurai Miyamoto Musashi stated that it is just as big of a mistake to be overly familiar with one weapon as it is to not be familiar enough with the weapon" This speaks of balance!

Chi Sao is a great exercise to develop the attributes outlined above, but it is not a panacea! There are several big mistakes I have seen in the thirty-plus years I have been involved with Wing Chun. One is an incorrect focus on the desired outcome of what the drill is intended to develop. Ip Man's eldest son, Ip Chun stated in one of my training sessions with him that Chi Sao is for development of the understanding of pressure and recognition of the opponent's use of force, and how to offset that force. It is also great for getting the student to build the habit of keeping the hands up in a position of protection at close range.

Chi Sao prepares the practitioner for "a moment in time" within a physical encounter, and specifically how to offset and react to the opponent's pressure when in contact at close range. It prepares the student for a worst case scenario, which is being at close range contact with an opponent and having contact with his limbs with your forearms and not with the much more preferable hands with which you can control his movement.

If given the choice, it is much better to grab, hold and control the opponent's arms with your hands than to be in contact with just the forearms and attempt to keep safe by keeping your limb in the way of the opponents punching line, which is essentially the skill that Chi Sao develops.

I have seen many practitioners of Wing Chun develop the idea that they will somehow apply Chi Sao in fighting, just to be unpleasantly surprised when their plan doesn't work out very well! You never, and I mean NEVER want to intentionally make contact with just the forearms when you could control with the hands!

The next mistake I see is in the use of Chi Sao as some kind of challenge game played between People as a type of sparring. It's not unusual to see Chi Sao morph into a senseless and useless game of "Slap Sao" with students attempting to measure their manhood and skill. In a way Chi Sao is like the "Crack" of Wing Chun. Students enjoy the competitive "Got Ya" game and get addicted, spending hours on developing little "Tricks" to get through the opponents hands to score a shot.

Many instructors encourage this because they are relieved of the challenge of teaching something of practical use. They can sit back and collect tuition checks while their students waste precious training time slapping each other around. I was in Hong Kong in 2005 for the Wing Chun World Conference. There was a gathering at Sha Tien Hong Kong University at which hundreds of Wing Chun trainees from the many different instructors and Wing Chun families got together for a training session. I remember watching two "well known" instructors, who had some bad blood between them, get into a one sided slap fest in a Chi Sao session. The "mine is bigger than yours" was on full, embarrassing display for everyone to see!

Chi Sao is not fighting. There are a lot of tools in the Wing Chun tool box that don't come into play in Chi Sao. In another incident, one evening in Foshan, China I was with my Sifu, Samuel Kwok and a group of his European students. We were supposed to visit a school that was of another Wing Chun lineage for a training and "Chi Sao" exchange.

The school was like something right out of a Shaw Brothers kung fu movie, with very impressive big traditional gates and a big boulder in the middle of the outside training area with the Chinese Character of Wu Shu (Martial Arts) carved on it. The schools master wore a short sleeved traditional jacket and was walking around manipulating a pair of Baoding Balls in his hand .... yea, those balls right out of one of my childhood favorite movies "Five Fingers of Death".

The atmosphere was very tense and unfriendly. If it weren't for the fact that everyone's mouths were actually synched with their words, I really would have thought I was in the middle of a kung fu movie! I later found out later that there had been some friction between my Sifu and the master of this school.

I remember Sifu coming over to me and saying "Be careful, this could get ugly" to which I responded " Sifu, if this is not a friendly get together, I am not letting anyone close enough to "play" Chi Sao. If there is going to be a fight, that's fine, but they are going to pay a price to get that close to me".

It is a mistake to do Chi Sao with someone who is unfriendly and has bad intentions. It is a no-win situation. If you go ahead and hit him, you are the bad guy. If you don't go ahead and hit him, you take a chance on him doing the same to you.

Fortunately Sifu Kwok's friend, who ran a martial arts supply company in Foshan, had accompanied us that evening. When the school's master attempted to get out of line, Sifu's friend, who, as it turned out was senior to that master in their kung fu family, put an end to his antics before it got out of hand! But I have to say, that is as close as I have been to a scene out of the old kung fu movies I watched as a kid!

One other mistake I see is the focus of Wing Chun training being too much on Chi Sao, once the attributes the exercise is designed to develop, have already been attained.

Sifu Massengill with his first Wing Chun teacher, Duncan (Shiu Hung) Leung, whom he trained with from 1979 - 1984 and Sifu Alan Lee on the right.

My first Wing Chun Sifu, Duncan "Shiu Hung" Leung, stated in an article in the magazine "Inside Kung Fu" in 1996, something that I heard him say many times in the years I spent training with him between 1979 – 1984. He stated that Wing Chun people do "too much Chi Sao". His point is that you don't fight with Chi Sao and that the ability to fight was the chief aim of training in Wing Chun to begin with. We have to keep the main thing the main thing! A little known Chinese student of Ip Man named Bruce Lee is quoted to have told a story of the folly of the man who carries a canoe on his back, after it has served its purpose of crossing the lake! We have to be cautious not to be weighed down by something that is no longer needed!

This should not be a strange concept to the student of Wing Chun. I have a very serious question for all of you out

144

there in Wing Chun land, especially those who are instructors. How much of your personal training time do you spend doing training drills like Dan Chi Sao (Single-Hand Sticking Hands)? Seriously, other than teaching it to students who are in the beginning stage of learning Chi Sao, how much of your personal training time is dedicated to this drill? My guess is, very little! And that is as it should be.

Why would you dedicate your precious training time, time spent away from your loved ones and other important things in your life, to train a drill from which you have already squeezed all usefulness? You wouldn't and shouldn't! You should be moving on to other things that help you progress towards your goal! Which should be efficiency in application of Wing Chun in a real fighting situation?

The same is true of Seung Chi Sao (Double-Hand Sticking Hands), once you have developed the knowledge, skills and abilities it has to offer, don't strap it to your back and let it weigh you down during the remainder of your training and thus, hinder your progress.

So the moral of this story is, train Chi Sao to develop what it is intended to develop. Develop those attributes, then move on and apply those attributes to other training more in line with the way you will be applying your skills in a violent encounter.

Chapter 13

Keeping the Main Thing the Main Thing

Several years ago I was invited to teach a seminar where I was one of two featured instructors. I was teaching Wing Chun and the other instructor was teaching his interpretation of Bruce Lee's Jeet Kune Do.

The seminar had the "stated intention" of presenting the similarities and differences in the approaches of the two systems. This had been discussed before hand and was the subject that the seminar host had arranged.

The other instructor opened the seminar by teaching a pre-set technique flow based on the JKD "progressive indirect attack" principle. The technique flow had the students begin from long range with a lead-leg round kick or side kick to the opponents shin, followed by a lead hand Biu Gee towards the eyes to "draw the hands" which resulted in a Lop Sao, with a Back-Fist attack which finally reached a target.

When my session began, I pointed out that the concept of the "progressive indirect attack" as demonstrated in the previous session, was a good example of the differences in approach between Wing Chun and Jeet Kune Do. I went on to explain that it is a well documented fact that Bruce Lee was very competitive, and liked to spar. It has even been reported that he studied films of Muhammad Ali, which he watched in a mirror to see how it would look as a right side lead fighter would fight. But here-in lies the difference. That is SPORT fighting. The whole idea of a progressive indirect attack as demonstrated by the other instructor, was that of progressively working your way in from an outside distance. This suggest a stalking type of fight we only see in a sporting or sparring environment.

I went on to explain that in a real world fighting situation, if I am at an outside distance, and feel the need to close the gap on the opponent, I would not do so empty handed. I would pick something up and hit him with it, or deploy my ever present best friend, my tactical folding knife and close that gap. This is what I see as the major difference in the two approaches, Real World thinking vs. Sport thinking.

Unfortunately, the other instructor was not happy with me pointing this out, and he sat on the sidelines during my session, glaring at me and looking like he was chewing on a turd-brownie. I spent the remainder of the weekend looking at this guys "trademark" scowl. My beautiful wife suggested that it may be time to break out my dusty copy of "How to Win Friends and Influence people"!

Closing the Gap

People often ask the question "Since Wing Chun is a close range system, that is designed to fight from bridge contact, how do you close the gap into that range in a fight?"

Well the answer is quite simple......We Don't!

When given the luxury of distance between the aggressor and yourself, use that distance to your advantage. If he wants to hit you, that distance is his burden, not yours!

You see, we are talking about "Real World" application of Wing Chun in a "Street" encounter. We are not talking about sparring, sport fighting, or a "My Dik Sao is bigger than your Dik Sao" contest.

In the street, I do not want to close the gap.... I don't want to fight, Period! I want to avoid the confrontation if at all possible. So, if you want to attack me, the distance between us is your burden, not mine! In the street there are no "off limits" targets. So if you want to step in and punch me, I can just lean away, keep my face out of target range and break your approaching leg with my low kick....in Bruce Lee's words "Use my longest weapon against the closest target".

I cannot think of a single circumstance where it would be necessary to bridge a gap, unarmed, between myself and the bad guy in a real fight. If I determined I needed to attack the guy first from a distance, I would use a weapon appropriate to the distance...a low kick to an extremely vulnerable target...such as his knee, or pick something up in the area I am in and beat the bad guy with it until he reconsiders his desire to do me harm!

The truth is, violent encounters in the street seldom resemble a sporting contest with the two engaged in the fight circling each other with dancing footwork jabbing and feinting their way to a knock out combination. Real attacks are sneaky, surprise attacks that are extremely violent, and are usually at close range before the intention to attack is revealed.

Street attacks are usually sudden and violent.

So generally, there is no need to close the gap, because you will not usually have the luxury of a gap. The bad guy will generally be close enough for you to smell what he had for breakfast. It is this range that the bridging and "so-called" trapping methods of Wing Chun are designed to work. The 'real fighting" not "sport fighting" distance.

Bridging Drills

Training our bridging skills is a necessity. So in order to develop a sense of distance, and timing, we do utilize a closing the gap training method. Generally this involves putting on some protective equipment, and having one party, the feeder, deliver attacks like a western boxer, kick-boxer, karate, grappler or some other opponent. While the one training the bridging skill, defends, times, enters or intercepts the attack and creates a bridge and counter.

While some of the training drills we utilize sometimes resemble sport oriented distances, we look at sport oriented drills like you would look at taking a prescription drug. When you have an illness or condition that requires medication, you have to balance the benefit of the medication against the possible side-effects. You take the medication, but must be able to recognize the signs of any possible side-effects, so that you can discontinue the use of the medication should they occur.

Side-effects of sport oriented training includes, but is not limited to, sport leakage into the self-defense application of your system. We must be very cautious to not get into a mind-set that fails to take into account elements which are very important in a street encounter, but do not come into play in a sport or sparring environment.

These bridging training drills are used to develop certain attributes, such as distance control, timing, and the coordination of footwork with the defensive and offensive tools, which once developed will be plugged into our fighting method. You can look at this like when my old football coach use to make us do the tire run in practice. He didn't make us run the tires because there were going to be tires all over the field on game day, but to develop our leg strength, and stamina, which in turn would improve our performance during the game.

These drills are used in addition to Chi Sao, which will develop our skills for the extreme close range of a real encounter. And once we have established bridge, the skills developed in Chi Sao will come into play.

Chapter 14

Putting it Together

An **Inconsistent Truth!**
If we look at how Wing Chun is traditionally taught, we see how the defensive and offensive techniques are combined together with each other and with the footwork of the system to create an applied, functional fighting technique. for example, the Chain-Punch is combined with the advancing step to create a movement known as the Chase, or Straight Blast. No one denies that this combination of techniques is Wing Chun.

In contrast, Combine the backward turning step from the Chum Kiu form with the turning Lahn Sao also found in Chum Kiu, to create a spinning Elbow Strike, and there are many in the "Wing Chun World' who would burn you at the stake of Wing Chun sacrilege, while shouting "There are no spinning techniques in Wing Chun"!

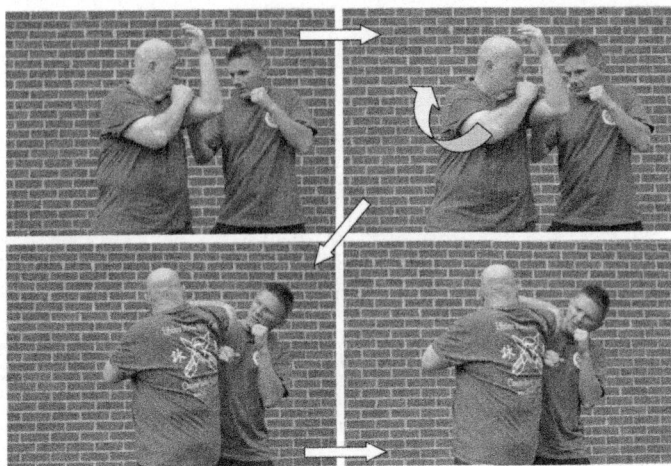

Purposely performing a spinning technique, when one that does not require you to turn your back to the opponent is possible, is not a wise choice. But there are times when the opponent may gain a superior position, and spinning may be the most direct, and efficient way to counter his attack. Wing Chun contains the tools for doing this job, but those tools often go unused because of the limitations people place on their application.

How is it that people do not see the inconsistency in this? It can even be seen in the almost total neglect of such tools as the upper cut and hook found in the second and third training sets of the system. People act as if the only punch in the Wing Chun is the straight punch. The conclusion of this kind of thinking is the limiting of Wing Chun, making it much less effective than it could be if we just unchain the system along with our creativity in looking at every possibility in our application of the tools of Wing Chun.

A new look at some old friends

If you were to visit a construction site, and pay close

attention to how the craftsmen utilize their tools, you may well come away with some new and very innovative applications to tools we have been using for years. A screwdriver for example can be used as a chisel, a pry bar, an extension tool to help drive a nail with a hammer in an area where the hammer can't reach the nail, a wood splitter, a weapon (nothing says "Leave Me Alone" like a screwdriver in the eye!!) .. as well as for driving screws!

Like the screwdriver, the tools of Wing Chun are limited only by our imagination when it comes to application. Many other Chinese martial arts teach the concept that a single movement may have a several striking applications, defensive applications, and a grappling (Chin-Na) applications. Looking at Wing Chun with this kind of mind set can open up a world of possibilities.

Looking at Wing Chun, Unchained from our preconceptions of what each technique is, and looking instead for "What All It Can Be" we are able to see where many practitioners have limited the system to a mere shadow of what it could be.

In this chapter we will explore some applications of techniques, with an eye towards some of the less obvious ways they can be utilized. In some techniques we may be looking at a different angle of use than is traditionally taught, in some we may be looking at a different contact point other than the way a technique is generally used. But in all if what we will look at, you will find their foundation in the tools of the Wing Chun system.

Footwork Unchained

Wing Chun footwork has as its foundation the Yee Gee Keem Yeung Ma, also known as Siu Lim Tao Ma. This is a base stance which is used as the main training stance of the system.

This basic stance teaches the student how to sink or root into their base. It is a measuring tool for the proper distance between the feet, and will be used as a means to check the stability and proper measure of the other footwork of the system.

The next footwork method taught is the basic stance shift, which helps the student to generate power in their technique and create proper structural alignment for the defensive and offensive tools of the system.

If the Wing Chun student were to stand in the center of a clock and perform the shift, the centerline will end up facing either one - o'clock or eleven o'clock. Once shifted and facing, in this example let's say one - o'clock with the center line, movement forward or backward will give the student four-direction balance. If the same person were to shift all the way to facing three - o'clock, and moved forward towards three - o'clock, there would be no side to side balance... it would be like moving on a tight rope.

So, we are shifted with our centerline facing one - o'clock. Our weight distribution is either 60% back leg, 40% front leg, or 70% back leg and 30% front leg, depending on who is teaching the technique. Wing Chun people don't seem to be able to agree on this matter.

I like what Grandmaster Ip Ching, youngest son of Ip Man, said in class one evening when one of my classmates asked about the discrepancy in the way this is taught. He stated "I don't carry a calculator to a fight - just keep all of your balance on the rear leg". I love the simplicity in the way Ip Ching approaches Wing Chun!

In moving with this footwork, the Siu Lim Tao Ma can be used to check on the movement of the footwork, to make sure we are consistent in the base we are fighting from. For example, if you step forward and punch, at the end of the movement, we should end up in the same stance. If our front foot moved 12 inches, our back foot should also have moved 12 inches, leaving us in the same base that we started out with. So if we shift the toes of the front foot back to the center, to a Siu Lim Tao Ma, we should be in the horse we always open up with in the practice of the first form. If we are more narrow than normal, the back foot is traveling further than the front foot in our step. If our stance is too wide, then our back foot is not traveling far enough in its step to keep a consistent base under us.

The stance and movement described above is classic Wing Chun, found in just about everyone's systems. The problem is that people act as if this is the only fighting foot-work in the system. This is great footwork. It is balanced and it has a strong foundational root. but it is designed as close range, bridge contact based footwork. With the majority of the weight rooted on the back foot, it is perfect for control when in bridge contact "Clinch" with the oppo-nent. But it is too rooted and stable "slow" for a fight outside of that bridge contact.

Look at Western boxing. Fighters like Sugar Ray Leonard were famous for their movement. His ability to slide in, strike and be back out of range before the opponent could react, made him a very hard fighter to beat. His ability to flow with the opponent when the opponent moved in to attack, and through foot speed, he was able to shift, slide and move just out of range of the opponents punch is almost legendary. He was able to do this because his footwork was mobile, not rigidly stable. He was light on his feet ..... at a distance. But when he ended up at close range, in clinching range, he became a rooted, flat footed fighter, because at that range he needed stability, not mobility. He knew the difference. Unfortunately, this idea seems to be lost among those in the Wing Chun world.

This is one area in which Bruce Lee, himself a Wing Chun student under Ip Man and Wong Shun Leung, was able to become very effective in his application of the Wing Chun he had learned. His footwork was much more alive than the "back foot in concrete" approach of most Wing Chun practitioners. When I see this footwork it reminds me of the Mummy movies starring Boris Karloff I watched in my youth. I remember, even as a kid, thinking how on earth does he catch the victim running from him when he is chasing while dragging his rear foot?

I personally believe that Bruce Lee's understanding of footwork and his subsequent exploration of western boxing and fencing was due in large part to his training with Wong Shun Leung. Wong Sifu had a background in Western Boxing, and understood the need for mobility.

If you watch Wong Shun Leung's footwork in the video "Wing Chun - The Science of In-Fighting" you will see his ability to move, angle and change directions is much different from what is taught by many Wing Chun instructors. I believe this was one of the key elements which made Wong the legendary fighter he became! But he did not add Western Boxing footwork to Wing Chun. If you know how to look at the system, it is already there!

In a fight, outside of bridge contact, mobility is much more important than stability. The ability to shift, slide, pivot and lunge is very important to your ability to defend against the modern mobile fighters we face today. The ability to quickly cover distance and exploit a moment of weakness on the part of the opponent can be the difference between victory or a visit to the local Emergency Room ..... or worse!

Let's go back to our shifted stance with our center line facing one o'clock. Now shift your body weight to a 50 / 50% weight distribution. In this stance, mobility will be much greater than in the traditional weight on the back leg "mummy" footwork. This footwork has its place, like Ray Leonard's rare flat-footed fighting moments, when in bridge contact (clinch) with the opponent, but it is basically suicide to fight this way at a distance.

Note that the only thing that has changed here is the weight distribution and your ability to move more quickly and freely. The base under your body is still based on the initial Wing Chun training stance.

Now let's take the same starting position and shift the weight to a 60% front Leg and 40% back leg with the knees a little more flexed and the rear heel off the floor with the weight on the ball of the foot. This you will find coincides with Bruce Lee's Bai Jong stance, and the Western Boxing stance. Same base under you, same distance between the feet, front to back and side to side. This position is nothing more than a different weight distribution, which creates a greater ability to move.

Transition from the traditional Wing Chun fighting stance, which is very stable and designed for close range fighting, can be made much more mobile with a simple weight distribution shift. Note that the base foundation of this more mobile stance is still the original training horse of Wing Chun.

This position allows for pivoting, and is much more conducive to the use of attacks such as the hook and upper cut, which are so often neglected by Wing Chun fighters..... Could it be that the footwork most of them use makes these weapons less effective and harder to use?

Each of these fighting stances has its place. Each has its advantages. Each has its range of use, and each draws its foundation back to the traditional stance taught in Wing Chun.

. . .

So Why is Movement So Important

There is a maxim in the fight game which states "You can't hit what you can't catch". There is a lot of wisdom to this saying. And if this is true in the ring ... and it is, just imagine how important it is in the street, where the cost of losing a fight is much higher!

Modern fighters are very mobile. This is a fact of life. Fighting methods have changed since Muhammad Ali hit the scene in the late sixties! Since that time the entire face of Western boxing has changed. If you look at boxing, pre-Ali and post-Ali you will see a vast difference in strategy and tactics. Does it not make sense that if the way boxers approach fighting has changed so much since the late sixties and early seventies, the approach to applying Wing Chun in this new fighting world needs to change as well?

Bruce Lee found this to be such an important factor in fighting that he highlighted movement as the component which gave his character an advantage over his more rigid opponents in several of his movies. A good example is in the movie "Return of the Dragon", during the fight scene with Chuck Norris, his character was losing, until he adapted a more mobile fighting style. This confounded his opponent, who up until this time had faced very little resistance to his attacks. By adapting a more mobile fighting method, Lee demonstrated how Norris's more rigid method was inferior. Norris eventually attempted to mimic Lee's mobility, but he wasn't able to adapt. Which brings us back to the principle that you don't rise to the occasion, but sink to your level of training? This scene was a great example of this concept!

The footwork used by most Wing Chun people consist of having the majority of the weight resting on the back foot, and utilizing a step-slid (drag) method of advancing. This footwork, while good at close range, is very vulnerable to attack in the outside ranges.

Many years ago, there was a student of a very well known Wing Chun instructor who competed in a MMA event called the Extreme Fighting Championship. He was billed as an undefeated Wing Chun fighter with a record which had been made up by the promoters. This Wing Chun fighter had not fought in any MMA events before this one, and from what I was told by a classmate of his, had not trained against any grapplers. As you can imagine, it did not end well.

Strategically and tactically, he was unprepared. What struck me was his moving across the ring with his weight firmly planted on his rear leg, and the grappler shooting in and dumping him so quickly he didn't even see it coming. Pushing forward with his weight on that back leg, too stable to move or dissipate the grapplers advance, made him a sitting duck for the take down. It was a sad display of a classic mistake made by many in the Wing Chun world.

This "Mummy" dragging the back leg - footwork has to change, or we as Wing Chun fighters are destined for extinction in the world of mobility!

I cover this material in-depth in our Videos, Seminars and Distance Learning program. For information you can visit our web site: www. EfficientWarrior.com

Chapter 15

Chin Na

C hin Na - secret techniques hidden within the forms!

The Chinese martial arts have been in development for thousands of years. The methods developed during this time have become highly refined. Chinese martial systems are generally comprised of not only defensive blocking techniques, but attacking methods that are separated into four categories. These categories are methods of striking, kicking, locking and throwing.

As the martial arts spread from China to Korea, Okinawa, and Japan these elements became splintered. For example, in Japan, if one wants to learn the striking methods, they study Karate, for throwing, Judo, and Joint Locking, Ju-Jitsu or Aikido. As you can see, these methods are no longer the cohesive unit that they were in the Chinese parent systems.

Although with the passage of time, the Chinese origin of many of these systems has been lost or hidden, a look at the origins of the Asian fighting arts will give insight into the Chinese influence of the methods of other countries!

The original Okinawan translation of the word Karate was "China Hand", however the kanji used to write China was replaced by the sound-alike kanji for "Empty", thus changing the translation to "Empty Hand". Popular systems such as Shorin-Ryu Karate trace their origin directly back to the Shaolin traditions of China. As a matter of fact, Shorin-Ryu is the Okinawan pronunciation of the Chinese ....Shaolin Family!

In 1638, according to Patrick McCartthy, in his book "The Bible of Karate – Bubishi" which is a translation of an ancient Chinese text passed from master to student in China, and then later in Okinawa, There was a Chinese martial artist named Chin Yuanbin (1587 – 1671) who left China for Okinawa during the end of the Ming Dynasty. He was a martial artist skilled in the art of Chin-Na (Seize and Control). He gained employment in the castle of the Owari Daimyo. There he taught three well known martial artist, who in turn developed three schools of Ju Jitsu.

The influence of the Chinese roots is seen in Korea as well where Tae Kwon Do was preceded by Tang Soo Do, again translated as "China Hand Way". And as in Okinawa and Japan, the striking components split from the locking and throwing components which in Korea are found in Hapkido.

As can be seen from the above, outside of China, the different elements of Kung Fu, striking, kicking, locking and throwing, splintered into different disciplines, but in China, most systems retain some elements of each. Wing Chun has many of these tools, if you know where and how to look for them.

Wing Chun, being a method that has a primary focus of close range application, is rife with techniques that lend themselves to not only striking, but also locking applications. A single technique may well have a blocking application, a striking application and a locking application! The locking applications are called Chin-Na.

Chin-Na is the locking element of most Chinese martial arts. But calling it the locking element is an oversimplification. Chin-Na is a highly refined skill in itself, and encompasses Locking, Grabbing, Gouging, and Breaking. Chin-Na can be used to immobilize, throw or disable the opponent and is the key to effective striking and kicking.

Translated Chin means to (Capture / Seize) and Na is (Control). Thus Chin-Na is the Chinese art of capturing or seizing and control. This needs to be explained further. Chin can mean Capture or Seize. To many, these terms mean the same thing, but they are actually quite different in the way we in Chin-Na think of them. The term Capture brings to mind a police officer apprehending a criminal, and this is an accurate description of the way Chin-Na is used to bridge and gain control of the opponent's limbs. But seize is somewhat different, and equally descriptive of the method of Chin-Na. Techniques are often used to Grab (Seize) the opponents muscles, ligaments and tendons, Veins and arteries, as well as areas like the eyes. So to seize is to grab violently.

As explained earlier, Chin-Na is the forerunner to such systems as Ju Jitsu, Aikido, and Hapkido. For that reason, many of the techniques used may be familiar to students with experience in these methods. Chin-Na is also the foundation for the method used in many Law Enforcement agencies. Chin-Na is perfect for Law Enforcement use because the techniques give the officer the ability to affect the arrest of a violent subject with the maximum of control over the criminal, and the ability to use measured force.

While I understand the use of this measured force by law enforcement officers, I do not generally endorse this method with my students. Police Officers need to control a subject to affect an arrest. A civilian needs to defend themselves against violent attack to affect an escape! These are much different goals, with differing methodologies!

Suffice it to say that I teach the martial arts from the perspective of use in a violent street encounter with someone who is attempting to do you great bodily harm or cause your death. Due to this approach, my application of the techniques of Chin-Na as well as the other methods I teach is generally very violent, with the goal of the immediate neutralization of the opponent's ability to harm me and provide me an opportunity to escape! I half-jokingly tell my students that all violent encounters begin with my thumb in the bad guy's eye and end with my foot on my cars gas pedal!

A joint locking technique should have any one or a combination of three objectives. The first is to break the joint that is seized and locked. Second is to use the lock to place the opponent in a position where they cannot defend against a secondary attack designed to take them out of the fight, and third to run them into, over, or through something that can hurt them in the environment in which you are fighting, such as down a flight of steps, through a window or in front of a car! Sorry, but fighting for your life is a violent event!

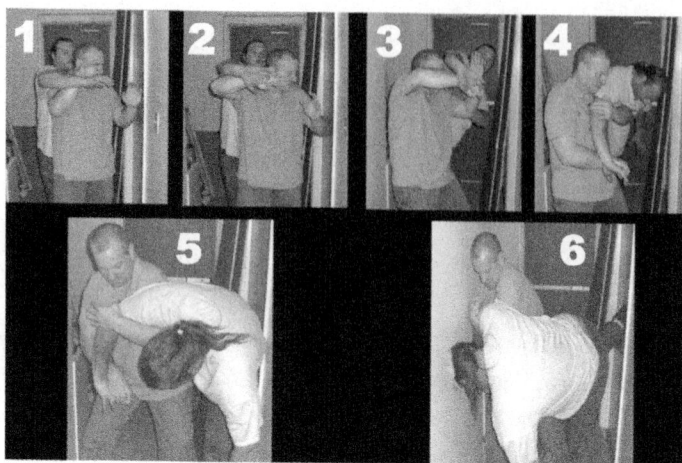

In a fight, we hit people with things and things with people! Chin-Na can help in controlling the opponent, and in utilising your surroundings as another tool in your arsenal.

All three empty hand forms in the Wing Chun system have seed movements for Chin-Na applications, but it is in the Chum Kiu form that the foundation of locking and striking applications are set. The second form is called Chum Kiu (Seeking the Bridge) or seeking a contact point with the opponent. In other Chinese methods this is called "linking" with the opponent. The concept has kinship with the Western Boxing defensive method known as the clinch. Whatever term is used to describe the method, the idea behind it is the same, to control the opponent and shut down his offensive options while simultaneously opening up an avenue of attack.

Some Chin-Na applications embedded in the Wing Chun forms are more obvious than others. One very popular method and drill in Wing Chun is Lop Sao. A Lop Sao is a grabbing hand, which is by its very nature a method of Chin-Na.

In Chum Kiu, what time instructors teach as the Jip Sao movement found in the first section between the double spreading Faak Sao (sometimes taught as a spreading Taun Sao) and the Chain Palm strike section is commonly taught as an elbow breaking attack. Most other Chin-Na applications remain hidden, but are treasures worth digging for.

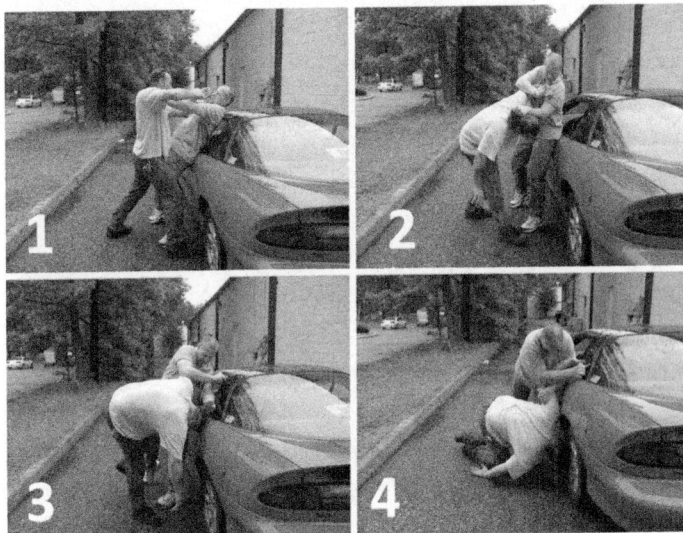

There may be times and situations in which it will be more advantageous to control the attacker and slam him into an object than to attempt to punch or kick him. The tools for this job can be found within the system of Wing Chun, when you explore with the mindset of cutting the chains of your preconceptions, and limitations of how to use the system.

To give one an idea of where to look .... A treasure map, if you will, let's look at some of the principles of Chin-Na application. With an understanding of these principles, you can examine the Wing Chun forms to find the seeds to Chin-Na applications hidden within them.

Chin –Na locks are generally applied to the smaller more vulnerable joints of the body. The joints of the fingers, wrist and elbow are the easiest joints to exploit, but the shoulder and neck are also targets of application.

Once contact has been made with the opponent, joints are attacked based on the easiest method of exploitation. If the opponent is in a tie-up position with you and has his hand open pushing against you, then his fingers may be the easiest to exploit! If he has grabbed you and his arm is straight, then his straight elbow is a prime target.

Joints are best attacked by applying force along two axis. For example, a wrist lock is much more efficient if force is used to twist and bend rather than by just twisting or bending alone. When you twist the joint, you stretch the ligaments and tendons to their limits, to add the bending of the joint after that will cause injury to be more serious and much easier to inflict.

Chin-Na techniques are applies through the application of any one or combination of the following:

Twisting
Bending
Hyper extending
Pulling
Pushing
Sinking
Raising
Compressing
Grabbing
Gouging
Separating

Rotating
And there are a number of other methods.

There will be situations and positions in which punching and kicking may not be possible. Chin-Na gives you options that may otherwise be unavailable.

To understand how these principles work, let's look at the application of Chin-Na finger attacks. Attacking joints generally causes damage by breaking the bone, tearing the ligaments, tearing the tendons or any combination of the three! Looking at the list above, the fingers can be attacked by way of bending, twisting, compressing, hyper-extension, separating, and several others. Again, any one or combination of the above will have the ability of causing great damage to the fingers, thus diminishing the opponent's ability to use the hand as a weapon, or hold a weapon with the hand.

There is a saying that states "Chin-Na creates striking opportunities and striking creates Chin-Na opportunities. The tactical benefits of understanding this statement are many!

A finger lock can be used to place the opponent in a position from which they will be unable to defend against your secondary attack such as a punch or low kick to the knee. When striking, when the opponent attempts to block, his blocking action presents opportunity to lock, which in turn opens new avenues for striking!

The hunt for the hidden treasure of Chin-Na applications within the Wing Chun forms can revolutionize your ability to dominate in a violent encounter, so break out your mental shovel and start digging!

I cover this material in-depth in our Videos, Seminars and Distance Learning program. For information you can visit our web site: www. EfficientWarrior.com

Chapter 16

Debunking the JKD Myth-Conceptions!

W hen a lie is told often enough.......it is seen as the truth!

In this chapter we will examine two areas where there are many misunderstandings, myths and outright lies in reference to Bruce Lee, his training in Wing Chun, and the development of Jeet Kune Do.

Let's begin with what this chapter is not. This is not an attack on Bruce Lee. I believe Lee was a genius in terms of his development as a martial artist and his ability to market his method. Secondly, it is not a knock on Jeet Kune Do. I have a lot of respect for the research and development of Bruce Lee's methodology. However, I have seen a lot of confusion and purposeful misrepresentation of the reasons for Bruce Lee's path of development.

My intention is to shed some light on the facts as to

Bruce Lee's depth of knowledge in the Wing Chun system, and his reason for the discontinuation of teaching the Wing Chun as part of his class curriculum.

WHAT WAS THE TRUE DEPTH OF BRUCE LEE'S FOUNDATION IN WING CHUN?

I have seen articles and web sites that make many claims as to Bruce Lee's training and level of knowledge and skill in the Wing Chun system. In these claims Bruce Lee's training time with Ip Man being up to eight years. I have seen the claim that Bruce Lee was one of the best fighters from the Wing Chun clan and other such statements.

These myths of Bruce Lee's exaggerated time under Ip Man are also propagated by movies like "Dragon – The Bruce Lee Story"

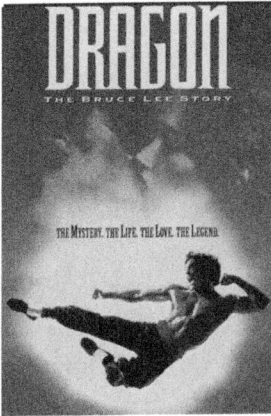

showing Bruce Lee in a training sequence, listed as being in Hong Kong 1949 that shows him as a kid so young he could barely reach the lower arm of the wooden dummy morphing over time into the nearly 18 year old Bruce Lee just before leaving Hong Kong in late 1958.

All of these things taken together paint a confusing and misleading picture of the depth of Bruce Lee's Wing Chun training. Let's see if we can shed some light on the facts.

· · ·

173

The following are some statements from some of Bruce Lee's classmates under Ip Man from Hong Kong and research from articles and books which may bring the truth to the forefront.

Here are some reference materials:

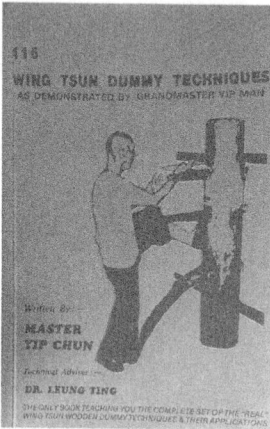

Ip Chun – from Book "116 Wing Tsun Dummy Techniques"

Pg. 109 "Before the end of the THIRD YEAR of learning Wing Tsun Techniques from my father, Bruce Lee had to suspend his martial arts lessons, for he had to leave Hong Kong for taking up academic studies in U.S.A.

Duncan Leung – From Inside Kung Fu Magazine November 1995

"Flashback-Hong Kong 1956, Fifteen year-old Duncan Shiu-Hung Leung is outside running on his balcony. Bruce Lee turned up in the street below. He yells he I got something new to show you.----
"Where did you learn this? I asked him – The technique

174

was "Chase Fist" He said: "had a new teacher he wanted me to meet. Sifu's name was Yip Man."

Ip Man 2 – Movie –At the end of the movie the following statement is made.

1956 – 16 year old Bruce Lee began Training with Ip Man.

Wong Shun Leung – Reminiscence of Bruce Lee – COPYRIGHT 1978

" One day, ABOUT 20 YEARS AGO, I practiced my Kung Fu in Master Ip's institute, I also helped my fellow learners in their practice. At that time, Chang brought in an Elvis-Like youngster. He leaned his body to one side with his hand on the wall. The other hand was in the back pocket of his trousers. His manner was very frivolous as though he thought that he was smart. I told Chang I did not welcome this young man.

A few months later, he came for a second time. But this

time he dressed properly and was more polite. Master Ip liked him very much, so he took him to be his disciple."

Pg. 41

"When Bruce started to learn Wing Chun he was a young lad. He was not a man of guts. But after he knew Cheung (Fellow Student William Cheung), he had time to drill his guts. In that period, he caused many disturbances. Both of them were about 16 years old."

Pg. 43

"Before Bruce went to the United States, he wanted to learn Chinese Northern Kung Fu so he could perform it on stage.....He thought some people might invite him to perform. He asked for my opinion. Of course I agreed with him. He had learnt Wing Chun for over Two Years, so he should be able to distinguish the kind of Kung Fu that was practical. He learnt it with a master for 10 days."

Bruce Lee's Hong Kong Years By Hawking Cheung as told to Robert Chu (From Inside Kung Fu Magazine 11/91)

Bruce said that his father would support him and pay for his expenses in the U.S., but he wanted to be independent. To make money on the side, he said he would teach wing chun. I replied that he didn't have much to teach at that time; we had both only learned up to the second wing chun form, chum kiu, and 40 movements on the dummy.

Chronicle of Ip Man's Life Article – The Timeline

1955 to 1957 (Man Kwok year 44 to 46)

Grandmaster Yip Man 62 to 64 years old.

Location: Hong Kong.

Grandmaster Yip Man moved the school to Lee Tat Street, Yao Ma Tei in Kowloon.

The students here were Lee

Siu Lung (Bruce Lee), Chan Shing, Haw Kin Cheung, Siu Yuk Man, Poon Bing Lid, Pang Kam Fat and others.

The Legend of Bruce Lee – Alex Ben Block (First Book on Bruce Lee

– Copyright March 1974)

(I believe this to be the most reliable text on Bruce Lee's actual training history, as it was written before the "Spin Doctors" began building the Myth that has become the accepted version of Bruce Lee's history.)

The following information was from interviews with Bruce Lee's brother Peter.

Pg. 21 – Bruce enrolled in the Wing Chun School and studied for the next TWO YEARS with Yip Man.

Pg. 23 – in the FALL OF 1958, with only $100.00 in his pocket, Bruce booked passage to San Francisco third-class on a freighter.

. . .

I believe these independent sources reliably place Bruce Lee's background in Wing Chun to be somewhere between 2 – 3 years, as a kid, age 16 to 18 years of age.

DID BRUCE LEE ABANDON WING CHUN?
Bruce Lee - Master of Bait and Switch

Now let's look at why Bruce Lee stopped teaching the Wing Chun aspects of his personal fighting method.

Normally when the terms "Bait and Switch, and New and Used" are mentioned, we think of car lots, not martial arts. But these terms not only apply to martial arts, they can be appropriately used in reference to Bruce Lee. Of course we will need to change the spelling of the word New, to Knew, because we will be discussing what Bruce actually "Knew and Used", compared to what he "Knew and Taught". This is where the terms "Bait and Switch" will come into play.

Bruce Lee arrived in the United States at the age of eighteen. He had no real job skills and very little money. Aside from his training in Kung Fu, he had very little he could do. So consequently he began teaching Kung Fu. Bruce's only formal training had been in Wing Chun Kung Fu. There has been a lot written over the years about the numerous systems from which Bruce created Jeet Kuen Do, many of these claims from J.K.D. instructors who have added to what Bruce had taught, and are attempting to sell what they are teaching as what Bruce taught. It has been acknowledged by Linda Lee, Bruce's widow, that Bruce's only formal teacher was Wing Chun Grandmaster Ip Man.

Bruce Lee was a very intelligent Martial Artist, and an

excellent Martial Art researcher, but the foundation on which Bruce built his personal expression of the fighting arts was Wing Chun. It is physically impossible for a building to be any stronger than its foundation. Bruce realized this, and used Wing Chun as the Foundation on which his life's work would be built.

JKD it has been said, is hard to define. In fact it has been so hard to define, that factions have formed within the ranks of those claiming to represent Bruce Lees "creation". Even with all of the confusion , among those recognized as experts in JKD, one thing can not be disputed. That fact is that Wing Chun was the foundation upon which Bruce Lee learned to view the world of fighting methods. His training in Wing Chun influenced every phase of his development as a fighter.

Ask yourself these questions. What made Bruce Lee stand out as different from all of the other Martial Artist in the 1960's? What brought people like Kenpo Black Belt, Dan Inosanto, and Heavy Weight Karate Champion Joe Lewis to his doorstep? Was it that he was teaching techniques such as Jab, Cross, Hook, and Uppercut, or was it his unique kicking methods such as roundhouse, side, hook, and back kick? The answer is NO. Everybody had those weapons at their disposal. The thing that set Bruce Lee apart from every other Martial Artist in the United States at that time was his knowledge of Wing Chun. No one else in the country had publicly demonstrated the Wing Chun system. What made Bruce Lee different were things he was demonstrating, such as Chi Sau (Sticky Hands), the Wing Chun principle of simultaneous defense and attack, The Wing Chun principle of Jeet (Intercepting) techniques. These were the things that made people who were already experts in other fighting methods seek Bruce Lee out for instruction.

When Bruce Lee first began teaching, he was teaching what he knew of Wing Chun. Because he hadn't completed his Wing Chun training before leaving Hong Kong, and because his teacher Ip Man refused to allow the teaching of Wing Chun outside of the Chinese people, as was tradition, Bruce called what he taught Jun Fan Gung Fu. Lee Jun Fan was Bruce's Chinese name. At that time Bruce taught a rather pure form of Wing Chun. In later years his teaching moved away from the Wing Chun and into a direction that more resembled a Kick-Boxing style. There has been much speculation as to why he made these changes. There are two events, which, I believe, clearly indicate Bruce's reason for removing Wing Chun from what he taught his students. The first was recorded by James DeMile, who was an early student of Bruce's. His recollection of that event was this:

(This is an excerpt from a letter from James W. DeMile to the editor and staff of Inside Kung Fu, and Hawkins Cheung. The latter who had a series of articles published on Bruce and JKD, to which resulted in the following reply.)

"What Sifu Cheung did not feel when he touched hands with Bruce's second- and third-generation students is some key elements that Bruce left out in his later teaching. Bruce made a statement to me that made everything clear as to why he changed certain aspects of his teaching. Jessie Glover, Bruce's first student and probably the best fighter in our group, and I were visiting Bruce when he was teaching a Jun Fan class in a Chinatown basement (Oakland). We noted that Bruce was teaching some things that seemed incomplete. We asked Bruce about this and he said, "Why should I teach someone to beat me?"

It was true. Why should he spend all his time developing his personal style and then give it away to someone else who might one day challenge him."

The second event was recorded in an interview with Dan Inosanto that was conducted by Black Belt Magazine.

(From Black Belt Magazine August 1995 p42-44)

BB: Were there certain topics you learned from Lee, but couldn't impart to other students?

INOSANTO: There were 13 things I could teach on the classical list, and that was it. He used to say that under no circumstances could I teach double Pak Sao (slap block). Pak Sao /Bil Jee (slap block/finger jab) and Pak Sao /Lop Sao (slap block/grabbing hand) were big big secrets. He was the head man, so I kept it exactly the way he wanted me to teach it.

NOTE: The restricted techniques were all PURE Wing Chun.

These two events clearly indicate that Bruce Lee made a conscious decision to discontinue the teaching of Wing Chun to his students, not because, as some have claimed, that the techniques and methods of Wing Chun were inefficient, but because he realized that Wing Chun was the thing that set him apart from everyone else. Indeed, Bruce knew that if all things are equal, such as knowledge, skill, and ability, then size and strength become a major factor. But if there is a significant difference in knowledge and skill, then size and strength can be overcome. If Bruce had taught students such as Joe Lewis, recognized by many as the most skilful and powerful Karate fighter of all time, all that he knew, then at 145 lbs, Bruce would have been at his mercy. In China, Bruce Lee was of average size, but in the United States, most of the martial artist that he came into contact with were much bigger, so secrecy became a necessity for survival. Thus began the Bait and Switch.

Bruce Lee commanded everyone's attention because what he was doing was so much different than the martial art systems that were then being taught in America. This difference brought people to Bruce's door. But Bruce was bringing people in with his personal method of fighting (Wing Chun), and then teaching these people something entirely different.

If the above isn't enough evidence that Lee never really moved away from Wing Chun in his personal fighting method, let's look at a few more pieces of evidence.

The 25 anniversary edition of Bruce Lee's Martial Arts epic "Enter The Dragon" contains some scenes which were unfortunately deleted from the original theatrical version. In it there is a scene at the beginning, right after the fight with Sammo Hung, where Lee is walking in the garden with his teacher. The teacher is questioning Lee about his thoughts on the Martial Arts. He asks "What is the highest form of technique"? Bruce Lee answers "To have no technique". The teacher asks him to explain. Bruce explains "A fight is like play, only played seriously. When the opponent expands, I contract. When he contracts, I expand. And when there is an opportunity, I don't hit....It hits all by itself!"

And as mentioned in Chapter Seven, Dan Inosanto, in 1980, wrote the very first definitive book on Bruce Lee's method called "Jeet Kuen Do - The Art and Philosophy of Bruce Lee" This was a widely anticipated book as it was written by the recognized head of the system after Bruce's death just eight years earlier. The first chapter in this book is titled "WING CHUN The NUCLEUS" Now I can't speak for anyone else, but in my mind, when the guy recognized as Bruce Lee's top student and the inheritor of the system he created, writes a book that calls Wing Chun the "the central and most important part of an object, movement, or group, forming the basis for its activity and growth" Which is the definition of Nucleus, then I have a hard time seeing how anyone can claim that Bruce Lee abandoned Wing Chun!

Finally, lets look at an excerpt from the book "The Tao of Gung Fu – a study in the way of Chinese Martial Art" by Bruce Lee.

The is a book published by Tuttle Press as part of it's Bruce Lee Library. This is a book that Bruce Lee wrote and intended to publish in 1965. Unfortunately it was never published during his lifetime. The book is primarily Bruce Lee's writings on Wing Chun. On pages 72 - 73, under the subheading "Close-Range Gung Fu – The Sticking hands Method of Wing Chun" Lee writes "Chi Sao is a flowing energy exercise in which we attach our hands to the opponent's hands and forget ourselves by following the movements of his hands, leaving our mind free to make its own counter-movement without deliberation. When the opponent expands, we contract, when he contracts, we expand – to fit our movements harmoniously into his attack without anticipating or rushing the action, but simply continuing the flow.

Note that in Bruce Lee's last movie, in an exchange in which he is explaining his idea of the highest form of technique, he is using the exact same wording he used back in 1964 to explain Wing Chun's Chi Sao!

I think this along with the above two examples builds a very compelling case that Bruce Lee never abandoned Wing Chun, but instead decided to keep his Wing Chun to himself as his personal "Secret Weapon".

Chapter 17

An introduction to Sifu Edmund Fong

Master Edmund (Wing Hong) Fong is a very well known teacher of the Ip Man / Ip Ching lineage method in Hong Kong. What is amazing is that many in the west are not familiar with him. He was a long time senior instructor under Ip Ching, as well as a board member at the VTAA.

Me with my Sifu, Edmund Fong, in Foshan, China 2007

I first met Sifu in 2005 while I was there to attend the 2nd World Conference and have had the great benefit of his instruction. He is, in my opinion the embodiment of the Ip Ching lineage of Wing Chun. It is my great pleasure to include this interview with him, in this book, to better introduce him to the west.

Sifu has recently (October 2021) immigrated to Canada, and will soon be making a much greater impact on the Wing Chun world here in the west!

Q: The fact that you lived in Hong Kong, you had an abundance of Wing Chun teachers to choose from, what is it that caused you choose Ip Ching?

I was influenced by Bruce Lee, and really wanted to learn Ving Tsun, so I tried very hard to find a Ving Tsun Sifu in order to start my training. I spent fifteen years learning from two different masters, but I felt that I could not apply what I had learned in the real world, but I did not know what was missing. At that time, there was no Internet, so I felt lost in my search. Until a friend of mine, introduced me to Sifu Ip Ching. I asked if Sifu Ip Ching would take a private student at his home, and he replied yes.

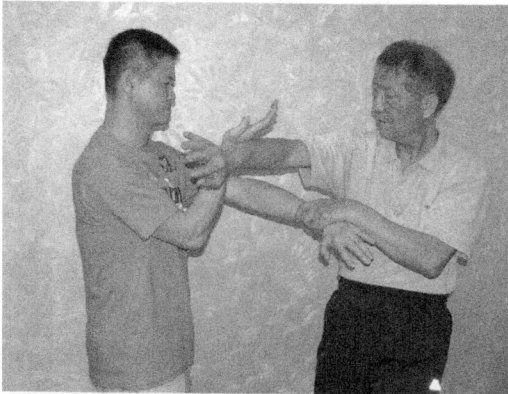

Sifu Edmund Fong with my Sigung Ip Ching

When I saw Sifu's kung fu in the first class, I was amazed, and I found that what I lacked, in my Ving Tsun, could be found from Sifu. I told Ip Ching that he would be my last Ving Tsun Sifu.

Q: For many years, you were the translator for classes your Sifu, Ip Ching, held with foreign (English speaking) students. You translated for seminars as well as for countless private lessons he conducted. Do you feel this unique opportunity gave you greater insight into Ip Ching's knowledge and teaching methods?

Yes, it was a great opportunity for me to learn more about Sifu's kung fu and his teaching methods. After the classes, Sifu and I would discuss more about the direction of teaching, and Sifu would tell me interesting stories about Grand Master Ip Man. So I miss those times very much.

Q: What are the most important points in your teaching methods?

The most important thing in my teaching is the movement structure and proper alignment, power generation and Fan Da Sau (Cycle-Attack).

Q: Forms, fighting application and chi-sao, what's the proper ratio in training?

I would say that the proportions are 40% for forms, 30% for combat applications and 30% for Chi Sau. The forms are the foundation, which teach the student the mechanical structure and power generation as well as Yiu Ma (Waist Energy). It is only when these are mastered that they can be applied to real fighting, and the same applies to Chi Sau.

Q: How does the Wooden Dummy fit into your training methodology?

The Wooden Dummy is very important.

Edmund working with his Sifu, Ip Ching on the Wooden Dummy, at Ip Ching home, Hong Kong.

In the preceding forms, the student is taught proper structure and energy of the techniques, but it is in the Wooden Dummy form that the student learns about the close range application of those techniques, as well as the use of footwork to gain the positional advantage over the opponent. Wooden Dummy training teaches the student to put it all together.

Q: In your opinion, how important is Chi Sao training? What do you feel it teaches specifically?

Many people think that Chi Sau exercises do not help in a real fight, and are a redundant form of training, but this is wrong. Chi Sau trains our hands tactile response to attack and defend during the practice, without the delay of having to think or decide. This is the result of Chi Sau practice. Wing Chun void of Chi Sao training leaves the student unprepared for application.

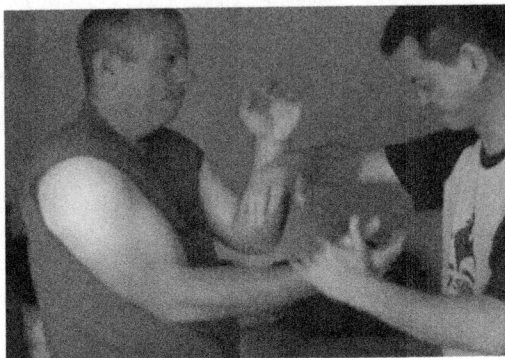

Training Chi Sao with Sifu Fong, Hong Kong 2005

Q: Does the weaponry aspect of Wing Chun (Long Pole and Bart Charm Dao) enhance the student's empty hands ability or are those two completely non-related skills?

The two weapons of Ving Tsun absolutely enhance the students' ability in fighting application. The Bart Charm Dao footwork is combat footwork. How can you flight without a good foundation in footwork?

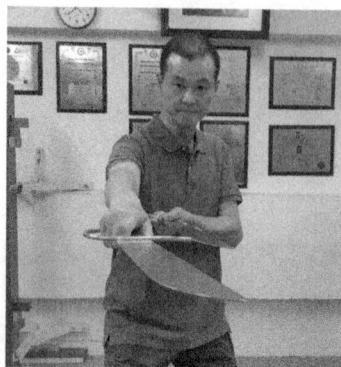

Sifu Fong training the Bart Charm Dao

The long pole is very effective in training elbow strength. But you have to practice it well. This is why the Six and a Half Point Pole and the Bart Charm Dao are so important to every Ving Tsun practitioner. However, many people only use their upper arms when practicing, this does not follow the principles of Ving Tsun.

Q: You were chosen to demonstrate a special Fourth Wing Chun form at the Second World Ving Tsun Conference in Hong Kong 2005. Why it was developed, who was involved in its development, and where did the idea for the set originated?

The National Athletic Committee wanted Ving Tsun to have a standard boxing form to represent the Ving Tsun system (such as the ones in Hung Gar, Choi Lee Fut and Tai Chi) Therefore, VTAA invited all Ving Tsun masters from all over the world to participate in the competition held in Hong Kong, so Sifu Ip Ching created the Chark Yiu form which was selected by the VTAA to represent Hong Kong in the Second World Representative Conference.

Sifu was in a tight schedule to create this form. Before the competition, Sifu asked me to come to his home to give my opinion. Sifu came up with the main idea for the 4th form, and he combined the most important parts of the three sets boxing form together. After watching Sifu's demonstration, I suggested that it would be better if other elements of the system could be added. So Sifu and I added the footwork aspects of the wooden dummy, kicking and knife to this boxing form, and then modified them to create the 4th boxing form (Chark Yiu). This is how the essence of Ving Tsun is expressed.

Q: In watching you perform Wing Chun, it is impossible not to recognize Ip Ching's DNA in your movements. The Ip Ching version visibly puts a lot of emphasis with the power being generated by the body, with looseness and flexibility.

Sifu Fong demonstrating with Ip Ching at the Second World Wing Chun Conference, Hong Kong 2005

Even the Chi Sao has a more relaxed multi-directional aspect to it, not just the "holding a ball" Bong and Taun Sao roll. Can you explain what that difference is?

Before I followed Sifu, my concept, in Chi Sao, was all about "holding a ball", but after I met Sifu, he never said a word about ball, because the longtime of Bong and Taun Sao roll would make the upper body shoulder tight and the arm muscles tense, so the freedom of hand movement was reduced. Chi Sau with Sifu feels like a dish of water that takes away all my power, and Sifu feels the flow of energy from his opponent. The main purpose of Chi Sau is to attack and defend finally, so Bong and Taun Sao roll should be short.

Q: You have a very long history in the Hong Kong Wing Chun scene. I know that for about ten years you served on the Board of Directors of the Ving Tsun Athletic Association, you run a very successful school, and are one of the most respected, and experienced instructors under Ip Ching. We first met in Hong Kong in 2005 and your reputation then was as a great instructor of the Ip Ching method. How do you feel about moving to the west where your reputation is not as well known?

I know the difficulties I will face this time when I leave Hong Kong for a new place, but I will insist on teaching properly, that is, to spread Ip Man and Ip Ching Ving Tsun to the next generation.

In Ip Ching's later years, he asked me to develop a systematic syllabus for teaching and grading. I will be bringing that system which was established in Hong Kong to the West.

Q: Can you tell our readers what made Ip Ching unique among all of the other Wing Chun masters you have met.

In addition to his excellent kung fu skills, Sifu is also a great teacher. He is kind and friendly, he is always willing to answer when discussing kung fu with me, he is never stingy, he will tell you what he knows, so that I can understand the use of each move and inspire me to have a deeper understanding of Ving Tsun.

Q: What are some of your future plans?

In 2005, Grandmaster Ip Ching formulated the fourth set form of Ving Tsun.

Edmund Fong demonstrating the fourth form, Chark Yiu, at the Second World Wing Chun Conference in Hong Kong

However, not many people know this form. I hope to spread this form to the world in the future so that more people will know the subtleties and benefits of this form.

About the Author

Sifu Tony Massengill

Tony is retired from a career in public safety where he worked for over twenty-five years serving as a police officer, fire fighter, and emergency medic. Over the span of his career he developed training programs and taught many in the field of law enforcement, emergency medical services, and the military.

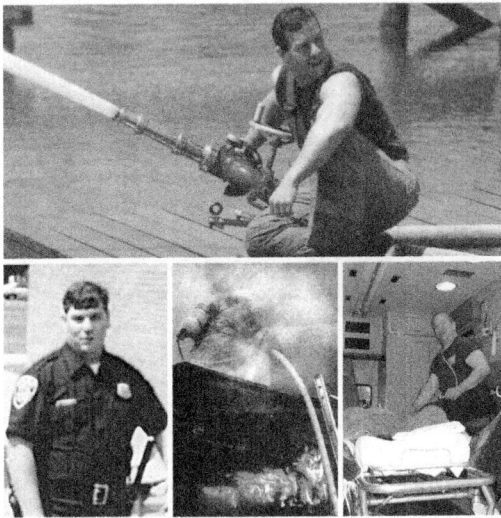

Massengill is a respected personal protection expert and consultant. He is the founder of Efficient Warrior Tactical, which develops and teaches programs in the area of empty hand, stick/blade and tactical firearms for civilian self-protection.

He has been involved in the martial arts for over fifty years, and has earned Black Belt rank or instructor certification in several disciplines, including Chin-Na, Kenpo, Tae Kwon Do, and various stick and knife systems.

Tony began training in the Wing Chun Kung Fu system in 1979. Over the years that have passed he has trained with several instructors, and was awarded Master level certification in the Ip Man Family Wing Chun Method in June 2005.

In 2013 Tony was honoured to have been included in the book "Wing Chun Masters by Jose Fraguas.

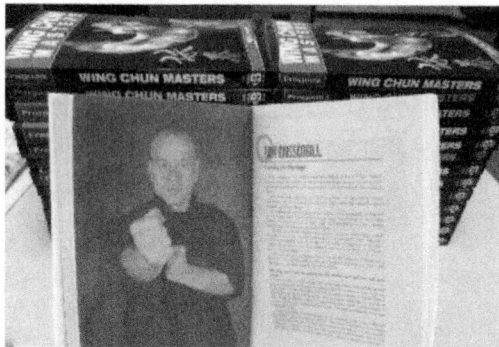

In addition to training with Samuel Kwok and Edmund Fong, Tony has also had the opportunity to train with his Sigungs, both sons of Grandmaster Ip Man, Ip Chun and Ip Ching.

Tony credits Sifu Edmund Fong, Samuel Kwok and Grandmaster Ip Ching with having the most impact over his knowledge and skill in the Wing Chun system.

Tony with his instructors, Edmund Fong and Samuel Kwok, along with his Sigung, Grandmaster Ip Ching.

Tony was selected to be Master Samuel Kwok's demonstration partner at the 2nd World Wing Chun Conference held in Hong Kong in 2005.

His first book, co-authored with Samuel Kwok was placed in the Ip Man Museum in Foshan, China in 2007. Tony was the senior U.S. Representative of Grandmaster Kwok and was appointed to administer Kwok's association in the United States, until his resignation from the association in 2010.

To date Tony Massengill has written four books, been featured in over a dozen instructional videos and written, as well as haven been featured in many numerous magazine and newspaper articles.

Tony resides in Hampton, Virginia U.S.A. and spends his time writing books and articles as well as teaching seminars across the United States.

FIRE/EMS
POLICE
911
27-Years
Practical Street
Experience Not Just
Theory or Sport!

Those interested in contacting Tony Massengill can visit his web site at: **www.efficientwarrior.com** or e-mail him at: **efficientwarrior@gmail.com**
Or call (757) 846-1188

Distance Learning and Seminars

Sifu Tony Massengill has a Distance Learning Program for those more interested in information on the ideas and techniques described in Wing Chun Unchained. He is also available for Seminars, within the United States.

For information visit our web site at:
www.EfficientWarrior.com
www.IpManWingChun.com

Also by Tony Massengill

Hard Target - Becoming Your Own Bodyguard

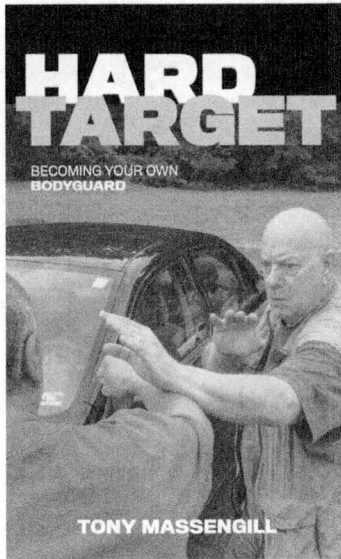

Traditional Wooden Dummy - Ip Man System

(Co-authored with Samuel Kwok)

Mastering Wing Chun - The Keys to Ip Man's Wing Chun

(Co-authored with Samuel Kwok)

Available at Amazon.com

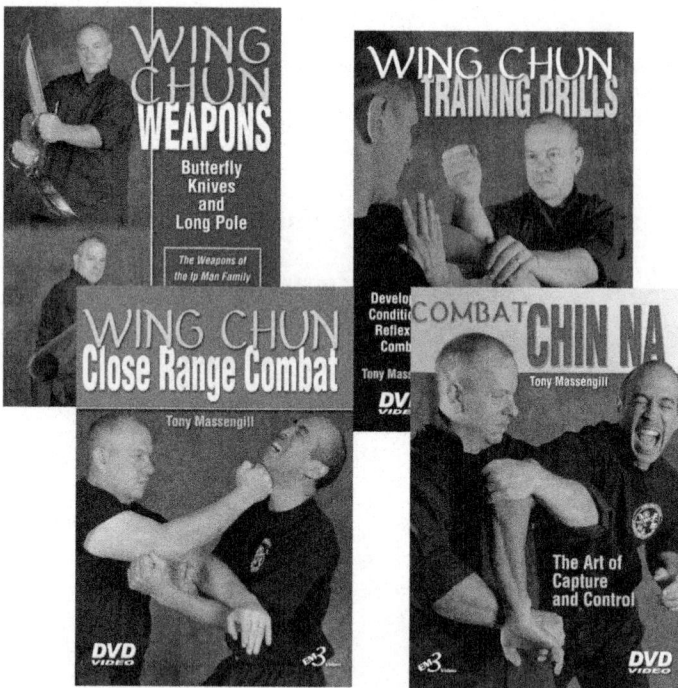

Sifu Massengill's Video Series - NOW AVAILABLE
For

DIGITAL DOWNLOADS

For Ordering and Pricing Information email:

EfficientWarrior@gmail.com

Or Call (757) 846-1188

Efficient Warrior Group

To find information on, or to become, a Certified Instructor and / or Training Group Leader please visit our web site at:
  www.EfficientWarrior.com or
  www.IpManWIngChun.com

We also highly recommend the Wing Chun and JKD books written by Jason Korol which can be found on Amazon.com

Printed in Great Britain
by Amazon